BELIEVE

*The Official Book of the
1997-98 Red Wings
Stanley Cup Championship*

The Detroit News

The Detroit News

MARK SILVERMAN, *Publisher and Editor*

JENNIFER CARROLL, *Managing Editor*

PHIL LACIURA, *Executive Sports Editor*

CHRISTOPHER KOZLOWSKI, *Assistant Managing Editor, Design/Graphics*

DAVID KORDALSKI, *Assistant Managing Editor, Presentation*

STEVE FECHT, *Director of Photography*

NOLAN FINLEY, *Manager of New Business Development*

EDITED BY: Rob Allstetter, *Deputy Sports Editor.*

COPY EDITING: Don Frost, Matt Rennie, Michael Katz, Terry Jacoby, Steve Wilson, Robert Jones, Art Brooks, Jeff Barr, Craig Yuhas, Duke Ritenhouse and Brian Handley.

GRAPHICS: Darryl Swint.

PRODUCTION ASSISTANCE: Karen Van Antwerp, Amy Chenail.

PHOTO EDITING: Steve Fecht, Ed Ballotts, Amy Kinsella and Steve Haines.

COVER DESIGN: Christopher Kozlowski.

BOOK DESIGN: Christopher Kozlowski and David Kordalski.

TYPEFACES: Giza, Bureau Grotesque and Village.

PRINTED BY: Grand River Printing & Imaging, Southfield, MI.

PUBLISHED BY: The Detroit News, 615 West Lafayette Blvd., Detroit MI. 48226 (313) 222-2300 and The Detroit Red Wings.

To Vladimir Konstantinov and Sergei Mnatsakanov.

Believe.

DANIEL MEARS

Dear Hockeytown:

We asked you to "Believe".

We wore the word on our chests. Initially, it served as a reminder to the team and Hockeytown — a reminder of how important Vladimir Konstantinov and Sergei Mnatsakanov were to our success last season and how important they are to us as family. As the season progressed, we realized that the word "Believe" came to signify many more things. And we asked you to believe in them all.

We asked you to believe that this team was up to repeating as Stanley Cup Champions. Please don't forget that we went 42 years between championships before winning last season, and we had some key losses from the team that ended the drought. But the intangibles that are so important when attempting to win the Stanley Cup Championship remained with us this season, as they were last season, and we added a few more along the way.

This is a tremendous hockey team, and I could not be prouder to be its captain. On the ice, these players work harder than any group I have been around. Off the ice, they are a first-class group of individuals whom I am proud to call a part of my family.

We asked you to believe in our young players. They turned their raw talent from promise into production.

We asked you to believe in our "grind line." They continued to provide their physically tough play and added a scoring power that surprised our opponents, but not our teammates.

We asked you to believe in our experienced players. Without their knowledge of the game, skill and leadership, we would not be champions today.

We asked you to believe in Chris Osgood. We knew how good he was. Now, everyone knows.

We asked you to believe in our coaches and staff. From top to bottom, we are led by the greatest coach of all time, two assistants who are simply the best in the game and a staff that gives their all and gives it from the heart.

We asked you to believe in Michael and Marian Ilitch. Success starts at the top, and our family ownership is unmatched in professional sports.

We asked you to believe in yourselves. The support we received from Hockeytown while playing in Joe Louis Arena, or any arena throughout the National Hockey League, continually inspired us through the rigors of a 10-month campaign.

Most importantly, we asked you to believe in the heart of a champion that dwells within Sergei Mnatsakanov and Vladimir Konstantinov. The challenges they face are far greater and much more important than any we face on the ice. They have shown us how to deal with adversity and how to strive to be the best we can be, no matter what the situation life places us in.

We often were asked if we were playing harder because they were gone. But they never left us. They never will. Vlady and Sergei were a big part of this team last season. They were just as big of a part of this team this season. Without their contributions, we might not have been able to keep the Stanley Cup in Detroit.

A year ago we were sitting in a room at Beaumont Hospital and doctors were telling us maybe Vlady and Sergei will live, maybe they'll die. One year later, they returned to Joe Louis Arena. They returned to Joe Louis Arena during this year's playoffs. And Vlady made it to the final game. He was on the ice with us, carrying the Stanley Cup. Our winning didn't help them return. But their returning helped us win.

We asked you to believe. And you did.

Now, we ask you to remember. This book will help you remember all the emotions, sacrifices and triumphs of the 1997-98 season. And it will help you remember the family, the Hockeytown family, that kept the Stanley Cup home in Hockeytown.

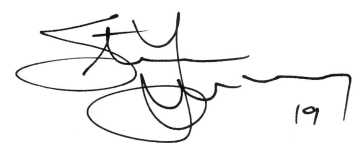

Steve Yzerman

They call it Hockeytown

BY LYNN HENNING
The Detroit News

H ockeytown, they call it. But the label, much like the current state of NHL hockey itself, has a certain 1990s marketing spin to it that isn't necessarily fair to Detroit. All the Hockeytown stuff does is tell us things about Motown (that used to be our name) we've always known to be true.

Such as, the matter of savvy. NHL experts understand that this is not only a town of hockey followers, but a region of sophisticated hockey students. Detroit's fans are different from most in that they know the game's nuances. They see the finer brush strokes that make hockey such a dimensional sports portrait.

Notice, for example, how many of the stalwarts with whom you gathered to watch this year's Stanley Cup playoffs could dissect a scoring play, or determine why a penalty wasn't called — and well before the video replay confirmed anything.

What it tends to underscore is that people here didn't just warm up to hockey because Fox television discovered it a few years ago (see: Dallas, Phoenix, Raleigh-Durham, etc.). Folks in these parts are born into a kind of hockey lineage. They tend to understand the game's heritage. Or, at least to the best of their abilities, they do.

For sure, we have seen during the last couple of years the flip side to Detroit's deep hockey roots. A walk along the parade route on the morning of June 18, 36 hours following Detroit's 1998 Stanley Cup Championship, told you that a lot of the crowd knew less about Jack Adams than about Sam Adams.

We have our profiles here, our demographic images, either of which will probably ring a bell:
■ Young woman, 20 years of age, long blond tresses, blue jeans, Shanahan jersey.
■ Young father, 25-30 years of age, holding onto the hands of his two small kids (sporting Osgood and Yzerman shirts), a serious expression on his face and a blood-red Konstantinov jersey on his back.

Whether either of these composite fans discovered hockey last year, or 15 years ago, isn't important. What's significant is knowing why and how they represent so much of Hockeytown 1998. And, how they differ from the group that comprised Detroit's 1950s, '60s and '70s fans, the older eras in Hockeytown's evolution.

JACK GRUBER

It is important to remember that Detroit has always owned an exclusive pedigree as a pure-bred hockey market. And while everyone might have heard about those high-voltage nights of yore in the old Olympia on Grand River Avenue, only those people of about 30 years of age or older have the foggiest idea what the old place was about.

Or, for that matter, what hockey then was all about. Or how, in 1998, it is so different. So very different.

On the morning of this year's downtown parade, Gordie Howe and old Red Wings teammate Johnny Wilson stood gabbing and laughing in the concourse at Joe Louis Arena. They would be leaving in a few minutes for their own place in the parade, but now, having made it past the early-morning traffic and crowds that had already turned Detroit upside down, two Red Wings stars from the 1950s heyday shook their heads at the phenomenon that was Hockeytown, 1998.

"Back when we played, our parade was from center ice to the dressing room," Wilson said.

Howe, his gray hair flashing, nodded and said: "I was talking with Sid Abel the other day, and he remembered a year when we won and the plane got home early in the morning. There were about 10 cars waiting for us."

What, then, explains the modern-day Wings mania? People line streets and expressways, taking off work for a victory parade. Joe Louis Arena sells out for "Joe Vision" of all things — a home arena filled with fans watching their team, on big-screen TV, play a road game. What about this craze of flying a Red Wings flag from your car? Of spending 100 bucks for a Red Wings jersey with a favorite player's name stitched on the back?

Howe and Wilson agree — the difference between Hockeytown then and now is the way in which a packed Olympia of 1955 evolved into a packed Woodward Avenue of 1998.

"Marketing," Wilson said. "The only one wearing a Red Wings shirt back then was a player."

"We had a red sweater with a Wing on it — that was it," said Howe, "and the public couldn't buy anything like that."

Marketing, though, remains a peripheral thing. Stanley Cup champions are about substance — about skill, and depth, and heart and soul. And it's that common thread that binds Hockeytown's old and new histories.

An hour before the 1998 victory parade kicked off, Darren McCarty, Detroit's hardnosed right-winger, stopped long enough in the Joe Louis concourse to shake Howe's hand and receive a hearty, "Nice going, Mac," from the man whom all but Wayne Gretzky's disciples believe is the grandest hockey player of all time.

Moments later, Sergei Fedorov appeared, looking sleek and electric in a black silk shirt that probably cost more money than Howe and Wilson received in bonuses for winning the Stanley Cup 43 years ago. How did it feel, Fedorov was asked, the second time around? What differences in emotions this year versus a year ago?

"Better this year," he said, instantly. "Back-to-back not easy to do. Last year, we were so desperate. This year, we already had a taste for winning. We had such experience. It tells us how good, how scary we are."

The rest of the NHL has no doubt had similar thoughts. All of which suggests the Hockeytown boom — to say nothing of jersey sales and car flags — may be a few years from leveling off.

Coach Scotty Bowman and Sergei Fedorov with the Stanley Cup.

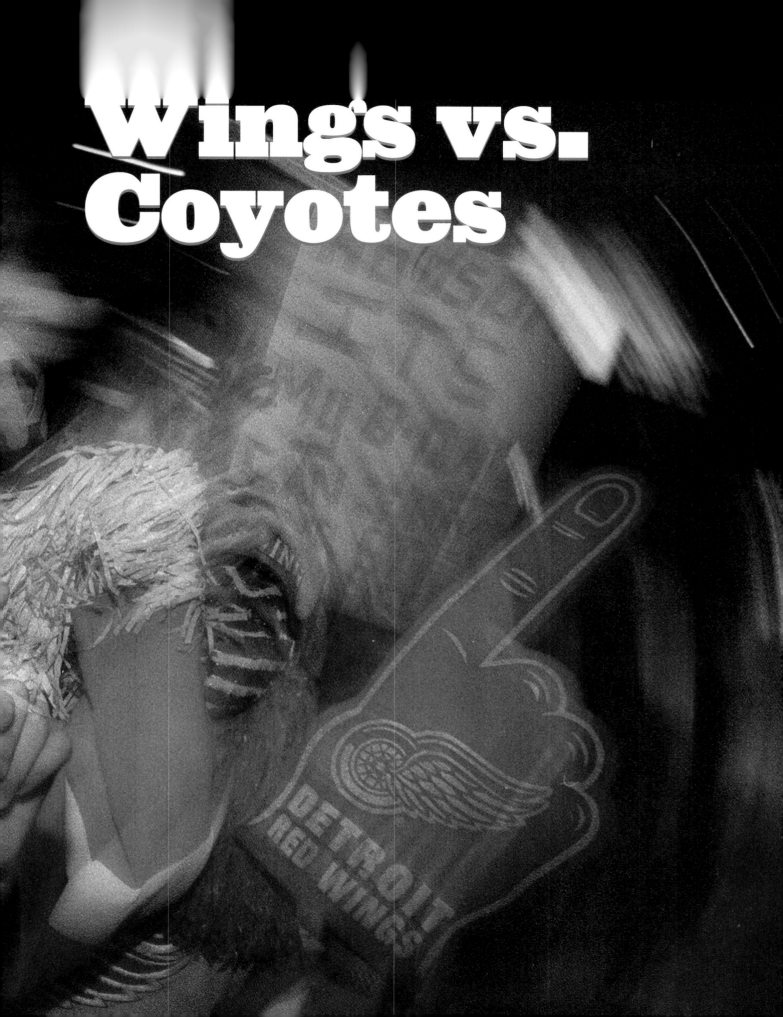

Wings vs. Coyotes

Sergei Fedorov helps bring down the Coyotes' Nikolai Khabibulin.

'Bulin Wall' crumbles

Grind Line powers past Khabibulin

BY CYNTHIA LAMBERT
The Detroit News

Do you know what happens when a grinder meets a wall? The wall falls.

That's what happened at Joe Louis Arena on Wednesday night, when the Red

WINGS	COYOTES
3	1
3	0
0	2
6	**3**

Wings' Grind Line combined for three goals in a 6-3 playoff victory over the Phoenix Coyotes.

The Grind Line — Kirk Maltby, Joe Kocur, Darren McCarty — renewed its heroics, scoring three goals and driving Nikolai Khabibulin from the game.

DANIEL MEARS

Martin Lapointe, right, replaced center Kris Draper on the Grind Line and stuck it to the Coyotes with two assists in Game 1.

The Grind Line was responsible for the removal of Coyotes goaltender Nikolai Khabibulin — known as the Bulin Wall — before the end of the second period.

"He had a tough game," Wings forward Martin Lapointe said of Khabibulin. "But you could see our guys and the way they came out. We raised our level up a notch, that's for sure. Right off the bat, we were there. You could see it."

The Coyotes were caught looking, and the game slipped away from them.

At 16:11 of the second period, Khabibulin was replaced by Jimmy Waite.

"We know that Nik can be better than that," Coyotes Coach Jim Schoenfeld said. "But the whole team can. ... Absolutely, (Khabibulin) will play the next game. He's our guy. He's going to have a terrific game."

Joe Kocur scored twice, his first two-goal game of the season, to lead the Grind Line, which became popular during the 1997 playoffs.

Grind Line center Kris Draper missed the game because of a sprained left knee. But Martin Lapointe replaced him and got two assists. Left wing Kirk Maltby also scored.

"I think the last time I scored two was (in 1991-92), when I was with the New York Rangers and it was against Detroit at Joe Louis," Kocur said. "I don't think anyone expects our line to provide much offense, so when we do, it's a bonus."

The last time Kocur had more than two goals in a season was 1992-93, when he had three. In 1991-92, he had seven.

Nicklas Lidstrom (power play), Sergei Fedorov and Darren McCarty also scored for the Wings.

Foolish penalties doom Coyotes

Red Wings deliver a stern message

By TERRY FOSTER

The Detroit News

Phoenix Coyotes goalie Nikolai Khabibulin stood uncomfortably while taking a series of questions from reporters in the visitors' dressing room at Joe Louis Arena.

The 'Bulin Wall' fell behind a team that looked like it was playing its season opener. The Coyotes were undisciplined and played dumb hockey in a 6-3 loss to the Wings in Game 1 of a best-of-seven Western Conference first-round series.

As the questions to Khabibulin subsided, someone asked him if his teammates had played undisciplined hockey in front of him.

His long pause and twisted expression said more than words. He was just too polite to say, "Yes!"

"We took some bad penalties, but we took some good ones," he finally said.

Talk about political correctness.

The Wings looked like the defending Stanley Cup champions, and the Coyotes looked like a Midget team.

"We played like a bunch of rookies out there," Coyotes right wing Rick Tocchet said. "We did not have poise out there, but we will be a different hockey club (in Game 2)."

The Coyotes had a nice game plan. They talked all week about being aggressive, scoring early and trying to take the crowd out of the game. It sounded good.

But they abandoned their game plan before Karen Newman finished singing the national anthem. They were penalized three times in the first 5:23 of the game. The Wings got a two-man advantage when Murray Baron was penalized for slashing, and eight seconds later, Nicklas Lidstrom scored to give the Wings a 1-0 lead.

By the time the Coyotes settled down, they trailed 6-1. They scored twice in the third period, but by that time, the Wings were thinking about Game 2.

"You can't give them four power plays in the first 10 minutes," Tocchet said. "It is like a slow death."

Said Coyotes Coach Jim Schoenfeld: "During the first two periods, we played a game completely void of thought and discipline. We could not do anything right, so maybe we squeezed it all out the first night."

Talk about dumb: Minutes after Cliff Ronning and Bob Corkum scored to help the Coyotes close to 6-3, Jim Cummins ended any talk of a comeback by getting called for a double-minor penalty.

Game. Set. Match.

Someone gave Coyotes center Jeremy Roenick a bogus scouting report. He talked all week about playing physical with the Wings, but his teammates did not talk enough about playing smart. You see, these are not the old Red Wings, who flinched with every hit and hardly raised a hand, even when opponents used to run at their goalie.

We all know about the Wings' speed and sleight of hand. But word did not filter to the desert about the Wings' power, toughness and spunk.

Roenick talked about a team that "does not like to be hit," but the Wings were in the work-out room lifting weights, riding stationary bicy-

Keith Tkachuk and the Coyotes put goalie Nikolai Khabibulin in an unenviable position by taking ill-advised penalities.

cles and preparing to punish the Coyotes.

No one told the Coyotes about the Grind Line. Joe Kocur scored twice. Kirk Maltby also scored, and Martin Lapointe had two assists.

The players who supposedly don't like to get hit not only took a licking, but hit back harder, until the Bulin Wall was nothing more than shattered brick and psyche.

"You hate to say they outclassed us, but they did," Tocchet said.

The biggest challenge for the Coyotes is to win the mental war. They played with passion, emotion and spirit. But the Wings, who have been through these types of games, channeled the Coyotes' energy against them.

"We did not have the discipline we need to win this series," Schoenfeld said. "It was a good lesson."

DANIEL MEARS

Blowout puts heat on Osgood

Those who know, know Wings aren't worried

BY BOB WOJNOWSKI

The Detroit News

COYOTES	WINGS
2	1
4	2
1	1
7	4

One by one, players stopped at Chris Osgood's locker, bearing apologies. They slapped him on the back, promised it would be different, pledged to give defense more than cursory interest in Game 3. Coach Scotty Bowman did the same, deflecting criticism from the Red Wings' goalie as if protecting a sensitive kid.

Osgood didn't want to hear it. An hour after the Wings' 7-4 loss to Phoenix Friday night, he stood outside the dressing room as bags were being loaded for the trip to the desert. He didn't have a white bandage around his head. His eyes weren't glazed, his mind wasn't fogged. He was fine, and he wished people would stop asking if he wasn't.

"I don't need guys consoling me, patting me on the head," Osgood said. "I have self-esteem. I know I'll play good. This is already forgotten. I can't wait for the next game."

In the playoffs, the next chance comes quickly,

TODD McINTURF

Chris Osgood watched the Coyotes celebrate a lot during Game 2.

Kirk Maltby creates traffic in front of the Coyotes net.

almost as quickly as the puck arrived in Game 2, fired by Coyotes who skated past Detroit defenders as if they were construction barrels with blinking orange lights. Inexplicably, the defending champs suddenly reprised the addle-brained Wings of a few years ago. Maybe they read the glowing reviews after their Game 1 romp. Maybe they got caught up in the skating and forgot the grunt work.

I do know this: Osgood needs protection, and

not the kind the Wings were offering afterward.

Listen. Osgood did not play well, which makes him exactly the same as virtually every other Wing except Sergei Fedorov, who continues to be the best player on the ice. But it's way too early to start whispering about "confidence problems," or for fans to derisively cheer when Osgood makes an easy save.

No team in hockey brushes aside misfortune like the Wings, and just because Osgood doesn't have

Tomas Holmstrom and the Wings were a step slow and a stride behind Gerald Diduck and the Coyotes during Game 2.

the fiery countenance of Mike Vernon, doesn't mean he's mentally fragile. It's hasty to start wailing, something owner Mike Ilitch should understand. Ilitch stood in the Zamboni tunnel after the loss and hurled criticism at referee Dan Marouelli, a display that should embarrass Ilitch, when he calms down.

The Wings are champions precisely because they control their emotions. So while others might lose composure, the Wings spit and grit their teeth.

The Wings actually controlled play for long stretches but committed monstrous concentration errors. Larry Murphy and Dmitri Mironov delivered tasty turnovers to Jeremy Roenick, who turned both into breakaway goals. The Wings need to crank up the hits, which is why Brendan Shanahan might

test his ailing back today, and why rugged Aaron Ward should be off the scratch list.

It's a long, hard grind, and if the Wings play as stupidly as they did in Game 2, it'll be a short, soft grind. The defense must be smarter. Osgood must make more big saves. But if you think one loss shocked the Wings or shell-shocked the goalie, you don't know your team.

"I don't want to make excuses," Osgood said. "I have to stop those pucks and I will. I don't worry about things. I'm fine. We have to win four and we will."

All psyches are intact. No one said this would be stress-free. Osgood has an early test, and to pass it, he'll need a bit more help from his friends.

DANIEL MEARS

Coyotes take lead on fluke

Loss is not the end of Wings, or Osgood

BY BOB WOJNOWSKI

The Detroit News

The puck hit Chris Osgood's left glove, rolled up his arm and dribbled down his left leg, on the way to the back of the net, on the way to nudging the Red Wings toward trouble.

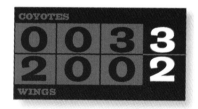

			COYOTES
0	0	3	**3**
2	0	0	**2**
			WINGS

JACK GRUBER

The Coyotes and their fans were all smiles after Jeremy Roenick's goal completed an improbable third-period comeback in Game 3.

Knowing the criticism that would follow, Wings goalie Chris Osgood watched Jeremy Roenick's shot — and with it, the game — slip past him.

It was the Coyotes' tying goal, fired from the blue line by Jeremy Roenick 2:19 into the third period Sunday, and it was a puck Osgood should have stopped. He knows it. The Wings know it.

Roenick knows it.

It was not, though, the end of the series. It was not the end of Osgood. If people want to label it the sole reason for the Wings' 3-2 loss to Phoenix, putting them in a two-games-to-one series hole, they'll do it without the help of the Wings, and certainly without the help of Scotty Bowman.

"Don't mess around, OK?" Bowman snapped when a reporter asked if the goal deflated the Wings, similar to the way Philadelphia was crushed by soft goals in the 1997 Finals. "We didn't have any deflation with that. That was Philadelphia, not here. That's my answer. Next question."

The goalie always makes the most glaring error. If the Wings had fought ferociously and Osgood's muff had killed their momentum, you would rightly blame it all on him. Osgood needs to make that save far more often than he misses it, but I don't believe the Wings suddenly turned mentally mushy, incapable of overcoming a mistake.

No, the problem right now is that the Coyotes are playing with a fury the Wings haven't matched. It starts with Jeremy Roenick and Rick

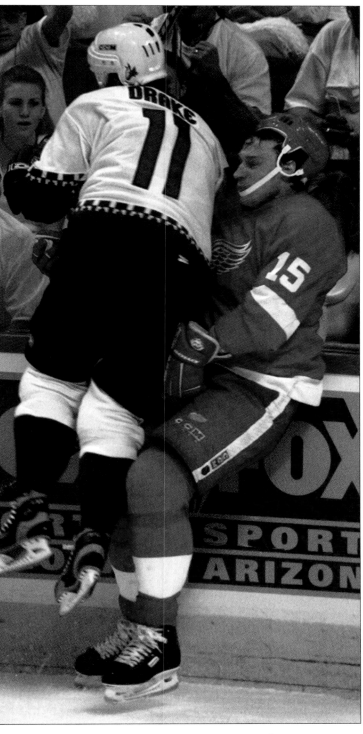

Dallas Drake leaves his feet to deliver a punishing check to Wings defenseman Dmitri Mironov.

Tocchet, veterans who are convincing the Coyotes they can play with the Wings. On the unscientific stat sheet, Phoenix was credited with 13 hits to Detroit's five.

The Wings tried to win with one outstanding minute, the game's first, when Sergei Fedorov and Brendan Shanahan scored. Playoff hockey is about momentum and emotion and the Wings let the Coyotes steal both by playing passively. Detroit's 0-for-6 power-play performance didn't help, and neither did the soft goal.

But if the Wings are being honest, they'll know their woes can't be pegged to one guy.

"I'm sure Ozzie would like to have that one back," Shanahan said. "But we can't worry about Ozzie's job. We're confident in him. If your team is deflated by one goal, or by failing to convert on a two-man advantage, then it's not playoff-tough. We've got to rise above that."

In the playoffs, one goal can turn a game, or a series. Ask the Flyers and Ron Hextall. It's not necessarily how many you surrender, but when you surrender them.

So Osgood needs to be better when it matters. And the Wings need to play with more passion. And everyone needs to avoid panic. And maybe captain Steve Yzerman needs to scold the troops, as he did when Detroit's series against St. Louis was tied at 2 in the first round in 1997.

Osgood, who calmly answered questions for 20 minutes, isn't shaken, even though he faced 32 shots, which used to be a two-game total against the Wings' stiff defense.

"I think I played like I can," Osgood said. "I felt unfortunate on that second one. The next game, I'll try to play the same, minus the second one."

Osgood entered these playoffs with the spotlight and the questions. After three games, the questions remain. On a day of squandered opportunity, Osgood lost a chance to steal a victory and bury the memory of Mike Vernon. But if the Wings aren't getting the big save, here's an idea: Go out and score the big goal instead.

JACK GRUBER

JACK GRUBER

Red Wing's get even

Aggressive play hold Coyotes in check

BY CYNTHIA LAMBERT
The Detroit News

Jamie Macoun beats Jimmy Waite in second period.

Now, it's a three-game series.

The Red Wings showed dogged determination against the Coy-

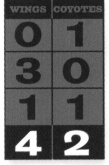

WINGS	COYOTES
0	1
3	0
1	1
4	2

otes in Game 4 to win 4-2 and tie the best-of-seven Western Conference series.

Tempers flared late in Game 4, once the Wings had control.

ALAN LESSIG

After the dust cleared and cooler heads prevailed, Wings goalie Chris Osgood took stock of the bizarre remnants of a hockey brawl.

"We played a lot more aggressive tonight," Wings defenseman Nicklas Lidstrom said. "We played better in front of the net. This is the way we hoped to play, the way we have to play in the playoffs."

The Coyotes lost more than the game — goalie Nikolai Khabibulin left midway through the second period because of a pulled groin and did not return. He is expected to be evaluated today, and his status for Game 5 is not known. Jimmy Waite, obtained in the waiver draft in September, finished the game.

The Red Wings also might have lost a player. Forward Brendan Shanahan was given a match penalty for intent to injure Mike Stapleton with a cross check with 4.3 seconds remaining. A match penalty is automatically reviewed by the league.

Coach Scotty Bowman vigorously protested the match call by referee Paul Stewart. Shanahan said the league will see in its review that there was no intent to injure.

"I didn't intend to injure him," Shanahan said. "He didn't go down, he didn't get hurt. Before that, I got a cross check in the back that I thought was unnecessary. I didn't agree with the call, but maybe he had a bad angle."

Igor Larionov, Vyacheslav Kozlov, Jamie Macoun and Lidstrom scored for the Wings. Rick Tocchet (power play) and Shane Doan scored for the Coyotes.

Two regulars returned to the lineup for the Wings — Martin Lapointe and Kris Draper. Lapointe missed Game 3 because of a pulled left hamstring, and Draper played for the first time since suffering a sprained left knee in the regular-season finale.

"Being down 2-1 in the series helped in my decision to play," Lapointe said. "I didn't want to regret the day if maybe we lost."

ALAN LESSIG

Hard work results in tied series

Wings learn from mistakes of past

By BOB WOJNOWSKI

The Detroit News

This was about getting pushed around and pushing back. Weary of watching Phoenix control play, the Red Wings went to work, heads down, skates grinding, and played as if they recognized the danger.

Sometimes, it just takes a little more sweat.

There was Tomas Holmstrom digging, digging along the boards, working the puck free from Bob Corkum, finding Sergei Fedorov, who fed Slava Kozlov for the go-ahead goal.

There was Martin Lapointe, delivering a huge hit, bouncing the puck loose toward the net, where Jamie Macoun slapped it in just before the second period ended.

And there was Chris Osgood, down to stop pucks, sliding to stop pucks, reaching to stop pucks, standing up exactly as he said he would after a shaky start to the series.

The Wings are back on their skates after a 4-2 victory over Phoenix, tying their first-round playoff series at two games apiece.

They showed desperation in the form of big checks, and Osgood turned momentum with big saves in the first period, when he withstood a ferocious Phoenix attack, an attack that withered

Tomas Holmstrom does what he does best — standing his ground in front of the opposing goalie.

as the Wings took control.

"One thing about the history of our club, we learn from our mistakes," forward Darren McCarty said. "We weren't going to sit back with the lead again. We tried to make hitting an issue and lay into some guys."

There are few secret weapons in playoff hockey, although Holmstrom, a bigger version of feisty Dino Ciccarelli, is becoming quite a pest. It usually comes down to puck control, and who's willing to fight for it. The Wings did, notably during a four-minute Phoenix power play in the second period. Clinging to a 2-1 lead, they killed the penalty masterfully, and just as the Wings' power-play failures had boosted the Coyotes, Phoenix's failure emboldened Osgood.

Now, the Wings can't let up, even though Game 5 is in Detroit, even though Phoenix goalie Nikolai Khabibulin left in the second period with a groin pull. Blood boiled in the final five seconds, when Brendan Shanahan received a match penalty for cross-checking Mike Stapleton from behind. It was retaliation, and it was the final blow in an increasingly chippy game, in an increasingly chippy series.

At least now the Wings seem inclined to chip back.

Darren McCarty helped the Wings tie up the Coyotes, whose hopes of taking a three-games-to-one series lead were dashed.

"We lost faceoffs, we lost battles in front of the net, we lost battles along the boards," Phoenix Coach Jim Schoenfeld said. "You can have your systems and your styles, but you have to work hard in the trenches and win the one-on-one battles, and they won most of them."

The roaring, white-clad crowd had sensed an open wound, chanting "Os-good!" to mock the Wings' goalie. The first period was all about weathering the white storm, and the Wings did, thanks to a toughening Osgood, who gave his team a chance. After allowing a Rick Tocchet back-

hander to dribble between his legs, he stopped Keith Tkachuk on a breakaway. He made a sprawling save on a 2-on-1. He began stitching together his confidence, save by save.

The Wings eagerly joined the rush. If they were to get any breaks, they'd have to earn them.

Bangers Lapointe, McCarty, Kirk Maltby and Joe Kocur leveled Coyotes. The Wings weren't about to let another lead slip away. They weren't about to fall behind, three games to one. A lot of work lies ahead, but at least the Wings have their sleeves rolled up.

Red Wing's stand tall

Detroit is a victory away from series win

BY CYNTHIA LAMBERT

The Detroit News

Mark Game 6 on your calendar because that is the game the Red Wings have a chance to clinch their first-round

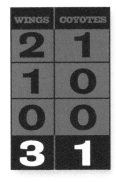

WINGS	COYOTES
2	1
1	0
0	0
3	**1**

Western Conference series against the Phoenix Coyotes.

DANIEL MEARS

Chris Osgood takes out some frustration on Rick Tocchet, who scored his sixth goal of the series for the Coyotes in Game 5.

The Wings put themselves in that position because of a sound, although not spectacular, 3-1 victory Thursday night to take a three-games-to-two lead in the best-of-seven series. If the Wings lose Sunday, Game 7 would be Tuesday night at Joe Louis Arena.

But with the way the Coyotes went meekly Thursday night, a Game 7 seems unlikely.

"Sure, we have some experience at these," Wings forward Brendan Shanahan said. "But we can't expect that because we've (clinched series) before, anyone's going to lay down their sticks and give it to us. Our experience is important and it's something we can draw on."

The Wings had a distinct advantage before the game began. Not only were the Coyotes without goalie Nikolai Khabibulin, but forwards Dallas Drake and Darrin Shannon also were scratched because of back spasms.

Yet, the Wings led only 2-1 after the first period. The score said more about Coyotes goalie Jimmy Waite than about the Wings' lack of offense. The Wings outshot the Coyotes 15-7 in the first period, and many of those shots were excellent scoring chances.

"I thought we had some good chances and he played them very well," Wings forward Brent Gilchrist said.

Tomas Holmstrom, Vyacheslav Kozlov and Sergei Fedorov scored for the Wings. Rick Tocchet (power play) scored his sixth goal of the series for the Coyotes.

"He's real good in front of the net," Wings goalie Chris Osgood said of Tocchet. "I try to look around him for the puck because it seems as though he's always in front."

DANIEL MEARS

Depth makes the difference

Wings' pests are equal to the test

By BOB WOJNOWSKI

The Detroit News

With the spring thaw comes pest season, as it always does in playoff hockey. It's when the swatters and squatters emerge, the guys who swarm to the net like bugs to the light. It's when teams with all the pieces start finding ways to win.

You can ride the stars just so long, a lesson the Red Wings are teaching, the Coyotes are learning. The Wings are shutting down Phoenix's dangerous players and finding new ones of their own, and with their 3-1 victory in Game 5, took control of their first-round series, three games to two.

The Wings' depth is wearing down Jeremy Roenick and Keith Tkachuk, and Phoenix's role players are powerless to stop it. This wasn't dominance, just brutal efficiency in front of goalie Chris

Nikolai Khabibulin doesn't like what he sees — another Wings' goal entering the net.

JACK GRUBER

Osgood. The Wings smothered the Coyotes so thoroughly, the game actually got boring, as Scotty Bowman likes it.

While Roenick and Tkachuk vanish, Sergei Fedorov, fresh and eager, continues to carve (dollar) figures in the ice. His goal, the game's third, was brilliant, as he faked Gerald Diduck right onto the highlight tape.

But Fedorov got help from his linemates, from guys who must emerge this time of year. It's time for the pests, for players who don't mind being hacked and whacked. It's time for guys such as Tomas Holmstrom. He wears No. 96, which makes him look broader than he really is. He's missing a key tooth, which makes him look meaner than he really is. He's not missing any guts, finding his place on a talented roster, finding his niche at the net.

Holmstrom was there, exactly where he's supposed to be, when Vyacheslav Kozlov ripped a shot that hit Holmstrom's stick and caromed past Jimmy Waite for the game's first score, and Holmstrom's first playoff goal.

"I feel very comfortable playing with Sergei and Kozzie," Holmstrom said. "Kozzie likes to shoot on net, so it's perfect for me."

Asked about his role, Holmstrom smiled.

"Pest?" he repeated. "I don't know. I don't want to get killed out there, but that's my game."

He also assisted on Fedorov's goal, becoming an unlikely cog on a speedy line. Bowman put Fedorov, Kozlov and Holmstrom

Sergei Fedorov, a holdout until late February, paid dividends against the Coyotes with goals worthy of highlight reels.

together precisely for the reason it worked. If you have someone willing to be abused at the net, you'd better have players who can get the puck there.

"Tomas has a lot of spunk," Bowman said. "He reminds me of (Esa) Tikkanen, a hard player to play against. He gets under your skin, but he also produces."

He also learns. Holmstrom caused a Fedorov goal to be disallowed in Game 4 because his skate was in the crease. Now he's running interference for two of the Wings' best skaters, a blocking back for Barry Sanders, a power forward for Grant Hill.

"It's like we each have our own favorite zone," Fedorov said. "And we always know where Tomas will be."

That's in front of the net, waiting for sniping from Kozlov, who scored the go-ahead goal. Guys such as Kozlov and Holmstrom are invaluable because they don't draw a star's attention. They're major reasons the Wings are one step from the next step.

The Wings took care of matters, not spectacularly, responsibly. They're pressuring Phoenix now, and acting as if they've been here. In the third period, a stuffed Coyote with a noose around its neck landed on the ice, and the crowd roared. The noose tightens, and Phoenix knows it.

DANIEL MEARS

Coyotes are erased

Wings power play dumps whiteout on Phoenix

BY JOHN NIYO

The Detroit News

This was no fluke, even if the final blow arrived Sunday. The Red Wings advanced to the second round of the playoffs with patience, the hallmark of a championship team, in a 5-2 victory over Phoenix Coyotes at America West Arena.

WINGS				
1	3	1		5
1	1	0		2
COYOTES				

The Wings won the best-of-seven Western Conference series four games to two.

Four Wings power-play goals — the last a bizarre pinball shot by Sergei Fedorov — were too much for the Coyotes, who skated with desperation and, as many expected, hurt themselves with ill-advised penalties.

"The penalties helped us," Coach Scotty Bowman said. "The only way you can cool down a team like that is to score some power-play goals."

If so, Fedorov's goal was the chilling blow. His dump-in shot took

JACK GRUBER

Brent Gilchrist slips the puck past Jimmy Waite.

Coyote defenseman Murray Baron and Wings center Brent Gilchrist try to fend off each other in Game 6. Gilchrist scored a big goal in the third period to clinch the victory.

a wild carom out of the corner, and the puck made a beeline for Coyotes goaltender Jimmy Waite.

Waite never saw the puck bounce off the back of his left skate and into the net to give the Wings a 4-2 lead.

Fedorov, who had six goals in the series, also didn't see the puck go in.

"All of a sudden the red light went on," he said, shaking his head.

The light went on, and the lights went out for the Coyotes. Steve Yzerman, who had a goal and two assists, said Fedorov's goal was a "back-breaker." Larry Murphy wasn't sure what to call it. Fate? Destiny?

"You can put whatever label you want on it," said Murphy, who set up Brent Gilchrist on a breakaway for the final goal. "We were just happy to see it go in."

The Wings weathered predicted flurries early amid the whiteout at America West Arena.

Jeremy Roenick scored on a power play to give the Coyotes a 1-0 lead at 7:03 of the first period. Yzerman tied the score at 15:28.

After Keith Tkachuk scored to give Phoenix a 2-1 lead early in the second, the penalties began to pile up — and pay off for the Wings. They got three goals, including two by Brendan Shanahan, to take control.

Chris Osgood, shown here being congratulated by Jimmy Waite, kept the Wings in Game 6 in the first period with many spectacular saves.

JACK GRUBER

Wings utilize man advantage

Power surge ends series

By BOB WOJNOWSKI

The Detroit News

You soften 'em with body blows. Bip. Bip-bop. Throw in a jab or two. Fwit, fwit.

Then, when they're weary and wary, when they have no idea who's coming from which direction, you hit with your best.

Steve Yzerman.

Brendan Shanahan.

Sergei Fedorov.

Oooph. Knockout.

On another White-Out Day in Phoenix, the Red Wings made it Close-Out Day, unloading with their stars. The defending Stanley Cup champs pride themselves on knowing their roles, and Sunday, the top players assumed theirs.

It's how you win games and how you survive tough first rounds, with goaltending and grinders and goal scorers. Don't ever forget the goal scorers. The Wings skated past Phoenix, 5-2, to clinch their playoff series, four games to two, largely because the Coyotes reverted to dopey play and the Wings' stars made 'em pay and pay and pay and pay, scoring four times on the power play.

Yzerman scored once, his first of the playoffs, and assisted on two other goals. Shanahan had two goals and an assist. Fedorov scored off a bizarre carom on a dump-in, with the puck bouncing off the left skate of goalie Jimmy Waite. We're not sure if Fedorov called the shot — Off the boards, off the foot, nothing but net! — but for stretches in a breathtaking second period, the Wings were taking target practice. The Wings are gathering momentum, the ol' red storm rising.

"Tell you the truth, I felt things were clicking when Brendan scored twice," said Fedorov, who had six goals in the series. "We feel like we're on a roll, but it's a very slippery road ahead. We're experienced enough to know that."

The power play won this game, but poise and discipline won this series. One thing about the Wily E. Coyotes, you give them enough Acme-brand twine, they'll hang themselves. All the Phoenix stars — Rick Tocchet, Jeremy Roenick, Keith Tkachuk — took penalties Sunday. The Wings had four consecutive power plays in the second period, when they outshot the flattened Coyotes (bleep! bleep!), 18-4. Meanwhile, the Wings' bangers — Martin Lapointe, Kirk Maltby, Joey Kocur — weren't penalized once.

The first round is about survival, and the Wings know it. They weathered the first period, then watched the Coyotes wither. Goalie Chris Osgood again kept the Wings in it with huge saves, and Yzerman was tremendous on the penalty kill when Phoenix, ahead 1-0, had a two-man advantage for 1:33.

Duly slowed, the Coyotes turned downright dumb. Tkachuk high-sticked Osgood. On the power play, Yzerman fired the puck from an odd angle and cleanly beat Waite. The captain was on the scoresheet, the team was on the board, the Wings were on their way. When Brent Gilchrist scored in the third period, he became the 13th Wing — an astounding total — with a goal in the series.

"They forced us to play our best to win," Yzerman said. "We got a lot of work on the power play. We got stronger as we went along. And we

Steve Yzerman, left, and Brendan Shanahan scored power-play goals to help end the Phoenix series.

played smart."

He smiled, wise not to say more, because as well as the Wings played in winning the last three, it can change rapidly, with this game as evidence. Every time the white-clad crowd got excited, the whistle blew, and another bad Coyote skated to the box.

"The power play is a gift you don't want to squander, and when we do, I take it personally," said Shanahan, who had one goal before Sunday but missed two games with back spasms. "The big-name guys put pressure on ourselves to score, but on this team, the big-name guys are also laying down to block shots. Look at (Yzerman). He does all the little things unnoticed by others, but not his teammates. It's contagious."

It's also eerily familiar. Things are unfolding nicely for the Wings, and people are noticing.

In the Phoenix dressing room, Tocchet raved about the Wings' leadership, starting with Yzerman but including such guys as Fedorov, who's playing the finest hockey of his career. Fedorov was everywhere, even as Roenick tried to shadow him, hit him, rattle him. Fedorov shrugged it off, then stood at the right point on the power play and retaliated the best way possible, by setting up goals.

The Wings had been 3-for-33 on the power play in the series and hadn't tallied a single success on the road.

"Phoenix was pretty aggressive, and the only way you're going to cool a team like that is to score on the power play," Wings Coach Scotty Bowman said. "Eventually, you have to win a game like this because teams are always going to try to slug it out on us. I wasn't worried. I never worry about our guys with big names. I know they can play."

They played with poise, and then, in the second period, they were stunningly efficient, as if they were tired of the silliness and ready to move on. The opening round is about weathering, about taking those first head-clearing hits. The Wings took it on and churn on, everyone contributing, stars rising at the right moments, as if they've done this before.

Wings
vs. Blues

Penalties leave Wings weary

Igor Larionov wears a bandage after his ear was cut by Chris Pronger's stick.

BLUES
1 0 3 4
0 1 1 2
WINGS

BY KEN KLAVON
The Detroit News

The way the Blues' Jim Campbell sees it, the team that stays out of the penalty box the most will win this series.

That's the lesson St. Louis Coach Joel Quenneville tried instilling in his team as the regular season dwindled down. So far, his team is listening.

Against the Kings in the first round the Blues were a potent 8-for-36 on the

OVERLEAF PHOTO: DANIEL MEARS; TOP AND OPPOSITE PHOTOS: DANIEL MEARS

Chris Pronger and the Blues knocked the Wings on their heels.

power play. They were equally effective on the penalty kill, allowing just one Los Angeles goal while shorthanded.

In a 4-2 victory over the Red Wings, the Blues again had more power-play chances than its opponent. Including a five-on-three, the Blues were 1-for-9. The Wings, also awarded a five-on-three, finished 1-for-6.

Wings associate coach Barry Smith stressed afterward how important it is to keep composure no matter the circumstance.

"You have to have focus. You have to focus that bad calls are bad calls and it happens every game," he said.

Smith was referring to several calls made by referee Kerry Fraser that had the Wings bench seething. The most crucial of the bunch occurred with seconds remaining in the second period. With the game tied at one, Brent Gilchrist was whistled for hooking. Then Steve Yzerman retaliated on St. Louis defenseman Chris Pronger away from the play as time expired. Before the Wings knew it, the face of the game had changed.

Eighteen seconds into the third period, Campbell popped in a power-play goal and the Blues had the momentum they seemed to have lost.

"I think game slipped right in third period," Sergei Fedorov said. "We didn't expect to get those soft penalties."

DANIEL MEARS

Simple remedy: Tie tongues, tighten defense

BY BOB WOJNOWSKI

The Detroit News

Maybe the Red Wings spent too much time around those mangy Coyotes and contracted that desert virus — temperamental viral stupiditis. Or maybe they figured referee Kerry Fraser was acting so cranky, they could, too.

More likely, the Wings' frequent displays of frustration during a 4-2 loss to St. Louis in Game 1 on Friday night were products of something much simpler: The Blues are pretty good, annoying in the way Eddie Haskell was annoying. They seem nice and nonthreatening, but by the end of the day, you've been duped.

The Wings were duped into dopiness, into taking foolish penalties, including some the helmet-haired Fraser actually called correctly. Let's get this out of the way. Fraser was awful. He fell for dives and missed obvious infractions, including Chris Pronger's wild stick swing that nearly left Igor Larionov looking like Evander Holyfield, post-Tyson bite.

But frankly, the Wings did this to themselves. They're trailing in the series entering Game 2 not because Fraser was bad, but because Pronger and the tight-checking Blues are good — and the Wings weren't ready for it, which was a surprise.

The champs generally don't get distracted. You could drop live octopi down their pants, and the Wings would keep skating. But there was Steve Yzerman taking a retaliatory high-sticking penalty on Pronger before the second period expired, setting up a two-man advantage that St. Louis converted. There was Martin Lapointe screaming at Pronger. There was Joey Kocur slugging Jim Campbell, then yelling at Blues tough guy Kelly Chase on the bench.

"I'm not going to harp on the officiating because we didn't play well enough to win," Yzerman said. "We were sloppy. We have to play tighter and at a higher tempo. The Blues are patient and they wait for their opportunities."

Scotty Bowman scolded the Wings for trying to hit home runs, while the Blues settled for singles. The Wings swung madly but whiffed, which happens. It was just odd to see, as the Wings took turns glaring at Fraser, then skating off for St. Louis' deadly power play.

"We retaliated and did things we normally don't do," Kocur said. "We realize what happened. And it's the easiest thing in the world to change."

Unglued ... uncharacteristic ... unconcerned?

No, the Wings should be concerned, because the Blues look faster and fresher, and are playing without star Al MacInnis, who has a groin injury. The Wings certainly can get smarter, but their defense can't get any younger, and it now seems the opposition's plan is to attack the Wings' defensemen, especially 40-year-old Slava Fetisov, and see if they're inclined to hit back.

For reasons unclear, the Wings often need a game or two to figure out what they're into.

They lost openers last year to St. Louis and Colorado. Some teams start tight and loosen up. The Wings start loose and tighten up. I suspect today they'll tighten their defense and their tongues, and kill that virus before it spreads.

Wing's awaken and belt the Blues

The scariest moment of the playoffs: Chris Pronger collapses to the ice after being struck in the chest by a puck; he recovered to play in Game 3.

TOP PHOTO: ALAN LESSIG, BOTTOM PHOTO: DANIEL MEARS

BY BOB WOJNOWSKI

The Detroit News

The whistle kept blowing and play kept stopping and tempers kept rising. Sticks and elbows were getting up; players were going down, and so many were marched off, they wore a rut in the ice to the penalty box.

All game long, menace hung in the air, with ugly stickwork, bloodied faces and one sickening moment when star St. Louis defenseman Chris Pronger took a puck just below the heart and fell to the ice unconscious.

The puck is a dangerous thing, and the playoffs are a dangerous time.

Thankfully, Pronger was resting comfortably Sunday night at Henry Ford Hospital, all X-rays negative, his heart beating normally, perspective imprinted on his chest in a purple welt.

"I'd never seen anything like it," said Red Wing Brendan Shanahan, shaking his head. "We're all trying to beat each other, we're all trying to bang each other, but that scared all of us. I think everyone on both teams, everyone in the entire arena, was rattled."

It was that kind of day, when the puck was bouncing crazily and fate was following. The Red Wings did what they

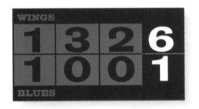

had to do, responding to danger by belting the Blues, 6-1, in a game that was far closer, tying their playoff series, 1-1.

On Desperation Day at the Joe, emotions broiled and the Red Wings struggled to regain composure against the St. Louis (Black and) Blues. There was so much grabbing and griping, you would have sworn it was Mutters Day.

The game and the series could have shifted either way, at any point, but amid the maelstrom, one Wing didn't flinch, the one who knows best the danger of the puck. Goalie Chris Osgood was spectacular, sliding left, sliding right, making a save on Pierre Turgeon when the game was 1-1 in the second period, altering momentum.

"A big save can turn a game around, like a big hit or a big block or a great shot," said Osgood, who made 24 saves to outduel legend Grant Fuhr.

"Every time (Fuhr) would make a save, I'd kind of laugh and say, 'OK, let's go, let's play.' "

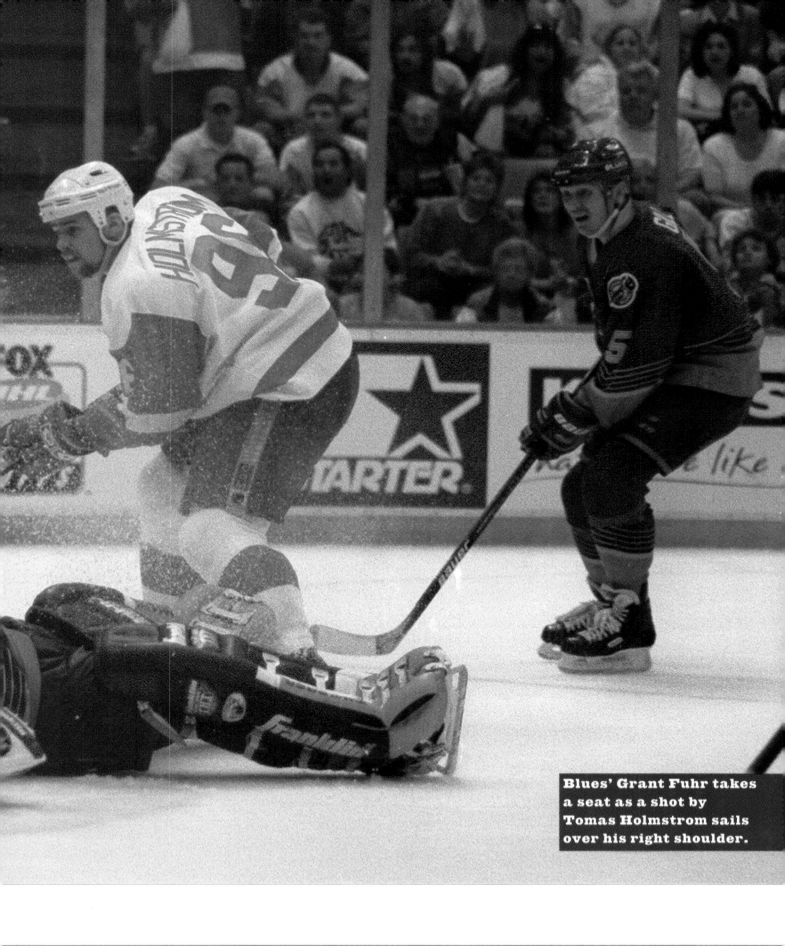

Blues' Grant Fuhr takes a seat as a shot by Tomas Holmstrom sails over his right shoulder.

Osgood was just as timely late in the period, when Pavol Demitra skated in alone and failed to beat him. In between, the Wings finally stopped taking penalties (four in the first period, none in the second) and started taking shots.

Nicklas Lidstrom scored. Tomas Holmstrom scored. Just when it was looking like Swede-est Day, captain Steve Yzerman flipped in a rebound and the Wings had cleared peril, taking a 4-1 lead.

Pronger's injury in the third period took the life out of the contest, but Osgood already had sucked the passion out of the Blues. If the series turned in this game, maybe the perception of Osgood turned with it. He bears the brunt of pressure in this

town, but in a raucous stickfest, he was cool and clutch, just like his counterpart had been in the Blues' opening victory.

"It's a weird feeling, like when we really have to win, it seems I'm more relaxed and more confident," Osgood said. "I got a couple of bounces that went my way. And I do have a little skill, just a little."

Osgood smiled, and it was nice to see at the end of an eerie day. The scene immediately after Detroit's Dmitri Mironov fired the shot that felled Pronger was horrifying, and way too familiar. The Blues' Brett Hull and Darren Turcotte saw Pronger's eyes roll back, and they raced to the tunnel to grab a stretcher, as doctors and trainers scurried onto the ice. If you wit-

nessed the Lions' Reggie Brown stop breathing after getting hit in a game last December, your stomach knotted watching this.

Within 30 seconds, Pronger was awake again, and he might even be back for Game 3 in St. Louis. The Blues, who didn't lose at home to the Wings all year, will need him, partly because their other star defenseman, Al MacInnis, is nursing a groin injury, and partly to restore emotion to a team that looked glassy-eyed afterward. Pronger had been the focus of the Wings' ire, and his huge presence was the difference in Game 1.

"When something like that happens, the last thing on your mind is hockey," said Blues defenseman Marc Bergevin, a former Wing. "It happened so fast, you just pray he's fine."

Even in Detroit's dressing room, the mood was odd. The victory was important, but almost every player admitted he'd never witnessed a scene as frightening as the image of Pronger prone on the ice.

The puck is a dangerous thing, capable of felling a 6-foot-5 defenseman, of befuddling a standout goalie such as Fuhr, of altering perceptions of Osgood.

With menace in the air and malice in the sticks, the Wings responded as you'd expect a champion to respond. It's not likely to get any easier against a St. Louis team that's strong and determined, but it can't get any more hazardous, can it?

Wings tie series at 1

BY CYNTHIA LAMBERT

The Detroit News

The Red Wings' first objective was to avoid falling behind two games to none in their playoff series against the Blues.

The second was to do some damage to the Blues' confidence.

The Wings appeared to accomplish both in a 6-1 victory at Joe Louis Arena to tie the best-of-seven Western Conference semifinal at a game apiece. The Blues lost for the first time in the playoffs — they swept the Los Angeles Kings in the first round.

"We got beat by a better hockey club tonight," Blues defenseman Todd Gill said.

It's a feeling the Blues don't want to get used to.

"They hadn't lost yet, they were 5-0," Wings goalie Chris Osgood said.

"We could tell they were very confident with the way their playoffs had gone. Even their third and fourth lines were confident. We played better today, but we can play better than that."

The series shifts to St. Louis for games 3 and 4 at the Kiel Center.

Terry Yake scored a power-play goal to give the Blues a 1-0 lead at 9:29 of the first period. Martin Lapointe (power play), Nicklas Lidstrom, Tomas Holmstrom, Steve Yzerman, Larry Murphy (shorthanded / empty net) and Kirk Maltby scored for the Wings.

"The score is irrelevant," Yzerman said. "The game was a lot closer than the score would indicate. Ozzie was great for us. In the first period, the Blues were coming but he was solid, he was great."

Sergei Fedorov helps Nicklas Lidstrom celebrate.

DANIEL MEARS

Overtime heroics doubly sweet for Shanny

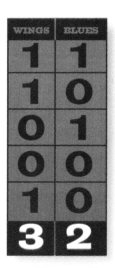

WINGS	BLUES
1	1
1	0
0	1
0	0
1	0
3	**2**

BY JOHN NIYO

The Detroit News

Al MacInnis and his hard slap shot returned to the St. Louis Blues' lineup for Game 3, and that meant a long night for Chris Osgood and the Red Wings.

MacInnis sent two of his familiar blasts past Osgood in Game 3 of the Western Conference semifinals. His second goal tied the score at 2 with 54.4 seconds remaining.

But the Wings escaped when Brendan Shanahan beat Grant Fuhr at 11:12 of the second overtime for a 3-2 victory and a two-games-to-one lead in the best-of-seven series.

"We deserved to win," Shanahan said. "We were proud of the way we played in overtime. I had a great (scoring) chance in the first period and that was on my mind when I was busting down the (left) wing (to score) in the second overtime."

The Blues thought they had won at 9:51 of the first overtime when Craig Conroy's shot from the right faceoff circle hit the right post behind Osgood and skidded along the goal line. But video-replay judge Jim Kehm ruled the puck never crossed the goal line.

MacInnis had missed games 1 and 2 because of a groin injury. Captain Chris Pronger, who collapsed in the third period in Game 2 after being hit in the chest by a puck, also returned to the Blues' lineup.

MacInnis showed why he was missed. He got a power-play goal midway through the first period to tie the score at 1. He tied the score at 2 with an 89-foot shot from center ice that went past Osgood. But he was apparently injured in the second overtime and limped off the ice.

Darren McCarty gave the Wings a 1-0 lead when he broke

Bredan Shanahan gives a yell after scoring the winner.

in and beat Grant Fuhr with a low shot. He tumbled over Fuhr and into the net after scoring at 3:10 of the first period.

MacInnis tied the score when he sent a 40-foot slap shot past Osgood at 9:15.

Tomas Holmstrom's goal at 1:36 of the second period — off a perfect drop pass from Vyacheslav Kozlov — gave the Wings a 2-1 lead.

Last shot outdoes Blues' long shots

BY BOB WOJNOWSKI

The Detroit News

When the Red Wings' Brendan Shanahan fired the puck past Grant Fuhr at 11:12 of the second overtime, the crowd gasped. It was almost as loud as the sigh emitted by Chris Osgood.

Shanahan, Detroit's Mr. Clutch, erased Osgood's last-minute flub, saving the goalie, the game, and maybe the series. The Wings played in overtime as if determined to right Osgood's wrong, and in the end, they got exactly what they earned, a 3-2 victory over the Blues that gave them a two-game-to-one series lead.

The deeper you go into the playoffs, the thinner the margins. A save here, an injury

Darren McCarty was flying high after scoring the first goal.

DANIEL MEARS

there, a penalty here, there and everywhere. One shot, one shift can turn a series, and with 54.4 seconds left in regulation Tuesday night, the Blues pulled out a dagger of hope.

Al MacInnis brought his big slap shot off the injured list and staggered the Wings with it, delivering a shot from the red line in the final minute that whistled past Osgood and sent

The St. Louis bench was singing the Blues when it was over.

the game to overtime.

These are the moments that test character, when you're less than 60 seconds from a hard-earned victory, when your defense is stuffing the Blues, who have had such trouble car-

rying the puck into the zone, they figure, "Aw, the heck with it, take a shot."

It was a longshot kind of night in St. Louis. A couple of blocks away, the Cardinals' Mark McGwire hit a 527-foot home run against Milwaukee.

McGwire does those types of things, and so does MacInnis, who scored in the first period on a power-play slap shot.

Now, we don't expect Wings personnel to spend today talking Osgood down from the top of the Arch. Osgood was excellent in Game 2 and was outplaying Grant Fuhr in this one. Osgood has had a tendency to fight the puck when fired by MacInnis, who might have the best slap shot in the game.

Was it a bad goal? Oh my, yes. The shot covered more ice than Sergei Fedorov does on a normal shift.

Will the Wings crumble because of it? Obviously not.

Will Osgood be affected? I doubt it.

For the bulk of the overtimes, the Wings dominated play, peppering Fuhr with scoring chances. Osgood was helped, too, by the narrow margins, such as the length of the goal line. At 9:49 of overtime, Craig Conroy appeared to win it for the Blues, but his shot hit the right goalpost, slid along the line and tapped the left post.

Between the drama at the end and the beginning, the game was, frankly, dull. The arena

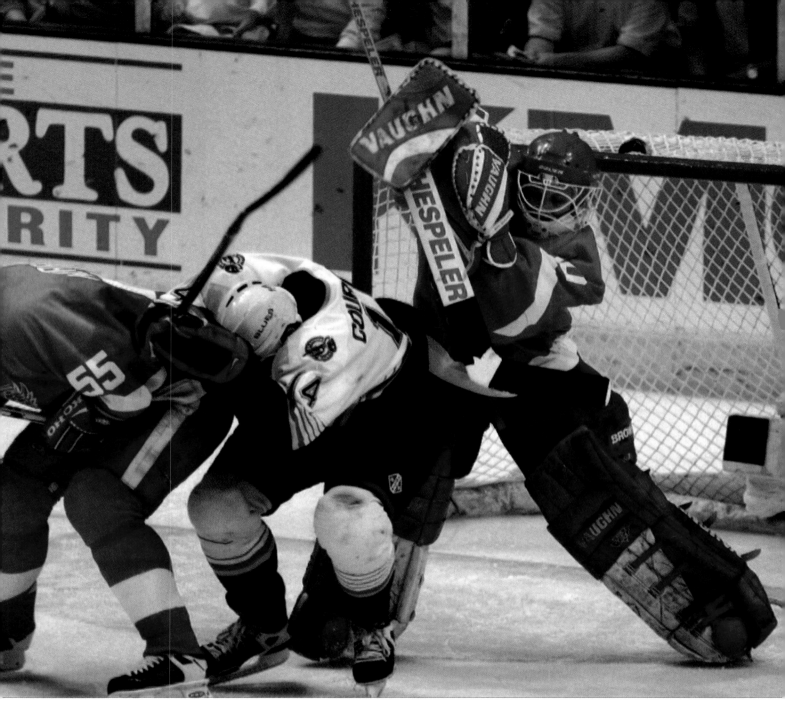

JACK GRUBER

was charged when Chris Pronger, who had collapsed after taking a puck in the chest two days earlier, took the ice for his first shift. He was followed shortly by MacInnis, who had missed the first two games.

It was a nice scene, and the good news for the Blues is that Pronger has a hearty heart. The bad news for the Blues was, the Wings have no time for mushy sentimentality.

Four minutes into Game 3, Martin Lapointe had clobbered MacInnis along the boards and Sergei Fedorov had jousted with Pronger. Oh yes, and Darren McCarty had scored a goal, then followed the puck into the net, bowling over Fuhr in the process.

Hockey is a sport of limited mercy. You back off, you lose. The Wings were staggered but fought back, and today, Osgood can breathe a whole lot easier.

Chris Osgood had to deal with company.

Blues on the brink

BY BOB WOJNOWSKI

The Detroit News

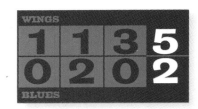

WINGS
1 1 3 5
0 2 0 2
BLUES

No sense waiting around. You see something, you take it, because you might not see it again.

The Red Wings see it now, squeezing the Blues before the underdogs get confident and start hitting the high notes. Sergei Fedorov saw it in the third period Thursday night, taking over a tie game with two goals and an assist, helping the Wings take over a series they probably can't lose now.

Detroit beat St. Louis 5-2 and has a three-games-to-one series stranglehold largely because they never let up, even when they couldn't get up.

Early in the third period, after St. Louis had erased a 2-0 deficit to tie the score, there was Fedorov, knocked on his wallet against the boards, controlling the puck from his backside, tapping to Tomas Holmstrom, who passed to Vyacheslav Kozlov, who deposited it behind Grant Fuhr for the winning goal.

"Sitting on ice, that is unusual," Fedorov said, smiling. "Holmstrom showed up at the right moment, and Kozzie showed up at the right moment."

Kozlov generally appears at such moments, late in close games, after the opposition seems to seize momentum. Pierre Turgeon's tying goal seven seconds before the end of the second period awakened an

Kris Draper helped the Wings establish a physical presence.

JACK GRUBER

ol' instinct in the Wings.

No sense waiting for the Blues to feel good about themselves and drag the partisan crowd along. The Wings outshot 'em 8-1 shortly after intermission, and settled matters quickly.

"We all realized we didn't play a strong second period, so we talked about it and regrouped," captain Steve Yzerman said. "Obviously, a goal right off the bat is really big because it allowed us to settle down. We find a way to get the timely goal."

They're getting timely at the right time. They've won three straight over the Blues, six of their last seven playoff games, four in a row on the road. And while the opposition tires and withers, the Wings get stronger, especially the center who sat out 59 games in a contract impasse.

Fedorov scored on a shorthanded breakaway midway through the third period, taking a perfect pass from Kris Draper, then added an empty-netter, proving what we suspected he would be — the difference-maker. St. Louis has no one to match him, and as the Blues' stars — paging Mr. Brett Hull — slip quietly away, Fedorov is everywhere, hitting opponents, hitting his stride,

Sergei Fedorov leveled Grant Fuhr with a goal.

JACK GRUBER

JACK GRUBER

hitting the jackpot.

We could make all sorts of cute references to his $12-million bonus, the one he gets if the Wings advance to the conference finals, but this is about more than money, and more than Fedorov. The Wings are getting help from all quarters, another goal from enforcer Joey Kocur, another fine game by Chris Osgood, who didn't crack as the Blues unleashed a barrage from every spot on the ice.

"Sergei's definitely the game-breaker," Draper said. "There's a lot of experience in this room and we're using it all to our advantage."

They're using it like a hammer on the poor Blues, who are turning purple in frustration. Osgood had stood in the dressing room the day before and declared himself mentally fit, while the Blues were down the hall, suggesting he gives up questionable goals on long shots. So Al MacInnis, who scored twice in Game 3, including the infamous 89-footer, shot the puck as soon as he stepped on the ice, and Osgood didn't flinch.

It's that time of year, when teams face off every other night, when weaknesses are picked at like fresh scabs. Tendencies are known, tempers are edgy and composure is key.

Speaking of familiarity, the Wings' Brendan Shanahan knows this town, having played in St. Louis for four seasons, and he knows this time. He scored the winner in overtime in Game 3, then opened the scoring in Game 4, beating Fuhr from a bad angle. That quieted the St. Louis crowd, as if it could get any quieter. (Blues fans are late-arriving, snore-inducing stiffs who occasionally were outcheered by a pack of 120 Wings rooters).

You need help from all areas, and that includes the grinders. So there was Kocur coming out of the penalty box, skating in alone on Fuhr and beating the future Hall-of Famer for a 2-0 lead. It was Kocur's third goal of the playoffs, and if that doesn't kick in a lucrative bonus, something's not right.

The Blues controlled the second period, getting goals from Jim Campbell and Pierre Turgeon, eliciting strong words from Yzerman and others during intermission. And here's the lesson of two games in St. Louis: The Wings might give up leads, but they don't let up. On the banks of the Mighty Muddy Mississippi, the Wings were more muddy than mighty, not that it matters.

They're faster and deeper, and when it counts, they have guys who put the puck where it belongs — in the back of the net.

Fedorov is the best player on the ice, but we already

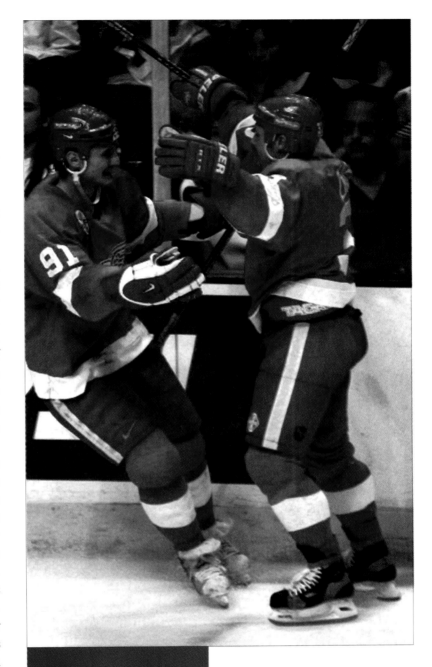

Sergei Fedorov and Kris Draper helped turn the game.

knew that. Yes, even with the fluky goal no one wants to forget, Osgood has outplayed Fuhr. The Wings are in command, and we could bore you with more details but you're probably busy rehashing the *Seinfeld* finale. So we'll just say, the Wings won as they always do, with stars and role players and ... you know ... yada, yada, yada.

The Wings did not welcome a return trip to St. Louis.

DANIEL MEARS

Wing's snooze, lose

BY BOB WOJNOWSKI

The Detroit News

The sun was shining; boats were churning through the river; country music fans were hoedowning in Hart Plaza. It was a beautiful Sunday in Detroit,

a fine day to kick the skates off, relax, maybe have a picnic.

So the Red Wings did.

Chris Osgood was busy, and without help.

Just when we were beginning to think the Wings were all computer chips and wiring, the hard drive melted and we saw the software. They're human, in case we forgot, prone to such basic emotions as complacency and laziness. And they put 'em on display in Joe Louis Arena, losing to St. Louis, 3-1, and committing the worst sporting sin.

The Wings awakened the dying, reviving the Blues, who trail the conference semifinals three games to two heading to St. Louis for Game 6. They pumped life into goalie Grant Fuhr, who was superb, making 29 saves. They let agitator Geoff Courtnall agitate again. And as for the Wings' power play, it's a powder play right now, two minutes of mayhem. They were 0-for-9 Sunday, 3-for-35 in the series, so I have a suggestion: When the Blues commit a

ALAN LESSIG

penalty, decline it.

The game ended in fitting fashion, with the Wings flailing futilely, pucks going wide, pucks hitting Fuhr, pucks sliding everywhere. The Wings had a chance to shoo the Blues, and they blew it, and they know it, and afterward, they were ticked about it, which is a good sign.

Pick your analysis, they all fit.

From Martin Lapointe: "They were limping and we had a chance to put them down and we didn't. We'll take the blame. We played awful."

From Brendan Shanahan: "Of course, we're mad. We had a chokehold on somebody and we let 'em loose."

From goalie Chris Osgood: "We pretty much lost that game the minute we came on the ice. You can't just go out there hoping to win. We went through the motions, and the longer they stuck around. ..."

One more analogy. You gotta kick a Blue when he's blue, and when the Blues left St. Louis down three games to one after the Wings' 5-2 victory in Game 4, the crowd was booing and the Blues looked like they couldn't get to the golf course quickly enough.

But after the Wings' stunningly tepid effort in the first period — that would be the complacency sin — the Blues figured, hey, Fuhr's playing well, we got a chance. They scored three times in 9:21 of the second

period, while the Wings sat around picnicking instead of nitpicking. The Grind Line of Kirk Maltby, Kris Draper and Joey Kocur wasn't hitting, and not until the third period did the Wings seem remotely interested in skating.

The thing about playoff hockey is, the door doesn't stay shut for long. The Blues were buried, supposedly, but one good period can lead to one good goal, which can lead to one good game, which can lead to one good chance, all of a sudden.

When Fuhr made a save on a wide-open Sergei Fedorov late in the first period, the door was cracked, and the Wings cracked.

"It's pride," said Fuhr in the dressing room, where the doomed Blues suddenly found themselves breathing freely. "Being dead and giving up, that doesn't work. The guys aren't going to surrender."

St. Louis is an experienced team, and it knew this series was closer than the records indicated. Of course, it wouldn't be closer if the Wings converted a stinkin' power play. Yes, they had scoring chances, so they're

not completely befuddled.

This wasn't a game Fuhr simply stole. Sorry. Too easy an explanation. It wasn't a game Osgood simply lost, either. All three goals were deflections.

The Wings played with no emotion, little energy and were sloppy, sloppy, sloppy, befitting a lazy Sunday.

The Wings generally respond well to adversity, and they are 2-0 in St. Louis, so I wouldn't

The Blues found a way to keep a lid on Tomas Holmstrom's production.

rip up those Western Conference Finals tickets. Picnic time is over. The Wings got soft instead of wary and it cost 'em. The good news is, they're mad about it. We'll see exactly how mad.

Red Wings cash in

WINGS				6
2	2	2		
0	0	1		1
BLUES				

BY JOHN NIYO
The Detroit News

The Wings have been down this road before. And it should come as no surprise that the landmarks are still there.

A goal from the Grind Line. A spark from Doug Brown. Timely scoring from Martin Lapointe. Solid play from a determined goaltender.

In Game 6, the Wings got all that and more in a 6-1 victory over the Blues to advance to the Western Conference finals for the fourth straight season.

Wings fans enjoyed their trip to St. Louis.

JACK GRUBER

Kris Draper and Darren McCarty know their next stop is Dallas

The Wings won the best-of-seven conference semifinal series, four games to two. They will open the conference finals at the Dallas Stars — and that leaves little time for celebrating, not that the Wings need any.

"A couple smiles, a couple chuckles and that was it," said Brown, standing in a quiet visitors' locker room after a workmanlike victory. "Now it's time to get ready for the next one."

The "next one" got a warning from the Blues.

"With all due respect to Dallas," Brett Hull said, "I really don't think they have a chance."

Hull, who can become a free agent, might have played his last game for St. Louis. But the Wings, who won all three road games in this series, proved they're nowhere near finished.

Chris Osgood (30 saves) weathered an early storm to anchor the victory. And Darren McCarty gave the Wings a 1-0 lead at 12:09 of the first period on a set play from Kris Draper off a faceoff.

Draper won the draw from Craig Conroy, sent the puck in front of the Blues' net and watched McCarty whack a shot that was deflected past a startled Grant Fuhr.

Tomas Holmstrom and Steve Yzerman sealed it with third-period goals, and Sergei Fedorov (one assist) earned a $12-million bonus because the Wings reached the conference finals.

"I don't care about that," Fedorov said. "We have a lot more hockey to play."

DANIEL MEARS

Blues can't match relentless effort

Wings' depth comes around in nick of time

BY BOB WOJNOWSKI

The Detroit News

Sometimes, it really is just a matter of time. Just a matter of time before the power play gets cranking, just a matter of time before the Red Wings get cranky, just a matter of time before someone rises from the bench when you most expect it.

Time ran out on the St. Louis Blues, eliminated in Game 6 because in the end, they didn't know which Wing was coming. There was Darren McCarty, back to his roots on the Grind Line, scoring the first goal. There was Doug Brown, back from the injured list after four weeks, scoring on his first shot, which had to leave the battered Blues muttering, "How much more do they have?"

The champs threw everything, skating with fire, desire and something familiar in sight — the Western Conference finals.

The Blues' sticky defense couldn't slow Darren McCarty.

For the fourth straight year, the Wings are in hockey's final four — an astounding accomplishment — set to take on rugged Dallas after belting the Blues, 6-1.

The Wings don't let opponents get comfortable, not for long. Two days ago, Grant Fuhr was brilliant, and the Wings were lethargic. This night, he was awful, while the Wings' Chris Osgood stepped up, right on cue.

All Osgood does is stare straight ahead, ignoring the public's obsession with him, making key saves.

By the end, Wings fans in the Kiel Center were chanting "We want Dallas!", and the demoralized Blues fans barely bothered to boo. The Wings do that to people, wear 'em out, because they're so deep, they can wait anybody out. Case in point: Brown.

He had a career season with 19 goals. Then he suffered a separated shoulder April 18, worked and waited, and has been ready to play. He was so ready, he nearly jumped out of his skates as he burst into the

Blues' zone and surprised Fuhr with a quick wrist shot for a 2-0 lead.

"It's certainly tough watching," Brown said. "But we have an attitude where, when guys jump in, they're ready to contribute."

If Vinnie Johnson was the Pistons' "Microwave," Brown is the Wings' instant offense (just call him "Brown and Serve"). He was scratched in the first round of last year's playoffs against St. Louis, then came off the bench and scored goals in three straight games against Anaheim.

You work and you wait, and you never know when your chance might come. There was Martin Lapointe, who unleashes his fiery style in the postseason. He scored twice, giving him five for the playoffs, and along with Steve Yzerman, was one of the best players all series.

His rebound goal sucked the breath from the Blues. It made it 3-0 and was one of three power-play scores, obliterating the Wings' 3-for-35 rate.

"We were (ticked) off, and guys needed to be (ticked) off," Lapointe said. "We showed what kind of team we are, when we want to be."

If you're the Blues, how do you weather it? You come in thinking you have to stop Yzerman, Sergei Fedorov and Brendan Shanahan, and you get hit by all these Lapointes and Holmstroms and Browns.

Brett Hull told the world that Dallas had little chance.

Wings stay focused away from home

Road warrior mentality

BY TERRY FOSTER
The Detroit News

They are no longer Red Wings.

Today I would like to introduce you to the Detroit Road Warriors.

Road Warriors wear blood-red jerseys over thick pads and skates. They don't simply walk into hostile arenas and win. They confiscate them. They demolish them and claim them as their own.

"You have experience here," forward Kirk Maltby said of his Wings teammates. "They are hungry, and they grab the bull by the horns."

We saw it again Tuesday night in which the Detroit Road Warriors tore up the former Kiel Center and renamed it Joe Louis West with a 6-1 victory. In winning three straight at the Kiel Center, the Wings, I mean

DANIEL MEARS

Warriors, claimed this best-of-seven Western Conference semifinal series in six games.

Appropriately, the Road Warriors begin the Western Conference finals Sunday at Dallas' Reunion Arena, which in a few days will be known worldwide as Joe Louis Southwest.

"After the game Brendan Shanahan told me, 'We smothered you. You did not have a chance,'" Blues forward Brett Hull said.

How good are the Road Warriors?

"With all due respect to Dallas, I don't really think they (the Stars) have a chance," Hull said.

Remember Grant Fuhr? A couple of days before this game, he was unbeatable. But Road Warriors eventually figure out complex equations and find weak links in what seem to be steel walls.

Someone figured out Fuhr was struggling to his stick side. Doug Brown, back for the first time in the playoffs after a shoulder injury, measured Fuhr and flipped a wrist shot to his stick side. Martin Lapointe followed. By the time Tomas Holmstrom ripped in a wrist shot, Fuhr was done for the game, lifted in favor of backup Jamie McLennan.

"I don't know what it is," Osgood said. "To be honest, we are more relaxed away from home. It is no secret. We just play relaxed on the road and play like we can and don't worry about anything."

Chris Osgood answered his critics again in Game 6.

Let's make this clear: Winning on the road is tough. Things are set up to favor the home team. The home team knows the ice, where the cracks are in the boards, and is determined to defend its turf.

"Everybody wants to play hard, and we are hungry for the puck," Lapointe said. "We play a lot better when our backs are against the wall."

Road Warriors simply become more desperate and more determined when everything is turned against them.

Road Warriors study and analyze. And when it is time to pounce, they're defining and deadly. Just ask the folks in Phoenix and St. Louis.

Wings vs. Stars

Defense dominates in Dallas

Wings beat Stars at their own game

BY DAVE DYE

The Detroit News

The Dallas Stars thrive on winning close, tight-checking games. That's what they got Sunday, but it came with a rude awakening. The Red Wings rolled to a 2-0 victory at Reunion Arena in the opening game of the best-of-seven western Conference finals.

WINGS	STARS
0	0
2	0
0	0
2	0

Dallas' Mike Keane caught Darren McCarty with his head down and hammered him to the ice in a highlight-reel check.

JACK GRUBER; OPPOSITE: DANIEL MEARS

A pair of captains, Steve Yzerman, right, and Derian Hatcher worked the boards behind the Dallas net.

Wings goalie Chris Osgood was sharp when he had to be, stopping 14 Dallas shots and befuddling Stars forwards such as Pat Verbeek.

Stars Coach Ken Hitchcock confirmed that his worst fears were realized with the Wings' dominance at what the Stars do best.

"This was an extension of their checking," Hitchcock said of the Wings' success. "Detroit has such a strong focus in that area. Their offense is really flowing from their good play in the defensive zone."

The Stars finished with the league's best record, but they really weren't much of a challenge Sunday. They advanced by beating the West's seventh and eighth seeds, Edmonton and San Jose, so the Wings were a big step up in class. Too big.

JACK GRUBER

In the last two years, the Stars did not make the playoffs and were eliminated in the first round. The Wings are playing in their fourth conference final in a row, and their experience was evident as they improved their road record to 6-1 in these playoffs.

"It's good for us to be starting on the road because of the way we're playing," Darren McCarty said. "We don't have to be stylish. It was the best thing for us."

The biggest difference between the teams is the Stars have almost no offensive threats other than Mike Modano, especially with Joe Nieuwendyk injured. Dallas relies on taking advantage of opponents' mistakes, and Detroit doesn't make many.

And when the Wings get chances, unlike the Stars, they know how to make them count.

Vyacheslav Kozlov scored a power-play goal in the first minute of the second period on a rebound

Martin Lapointe raises his stick in celebration after scoring the Wings' second goal off a setup by Jamie Macoun.

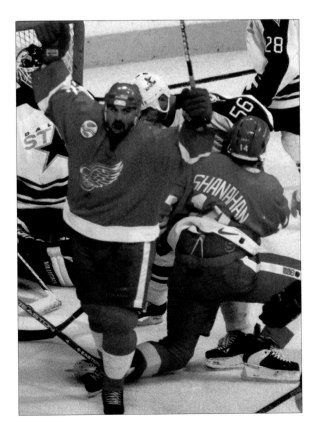

Vyacheslav Kozlov, left, popped in the Wings' first goal and got a hug from Martin Lapointe in the second period.

of Nicklas Lidstrom's wrist shot from the point.

Martin Lapointe scored the other goal later in the period when he was set up by defenseman Jamie Macoun.

Chris Osgood made 14 saves for his fourth career playoff shutout.

Road warriors

Simple statement: Any way, any place

By BOB WOJNOWSKI

The Detroit News

The Stars would wear down the Red Wings, that was the plan. They'd use their defense, discipline and patience and watch the Wings wilt in the slushy Texas ice.

Here's the retort from the Wings, delivered with startling simplicity Sunday: Whatever style you want to play, wherever you want to play it, pardner.

The Wings were using defense, discipline and patience when these Stars were hockey infants. So it's hardly a surprise they turned it all on Dallas in a numbing 2-0 victory in Game 1 of the Western Conference finals.

Sorry, but the Stars better bring something else and bring it soon, because if they're going to sit and wait for the Wings to make mistakes, they'll be waiting until the cattle come home. We knew this was the Big D, and it stood for Big Defense. But Big D and little o, very little o, aren't nearly enough to derail the champs.

The Wings can play defense with anyone; they just don't advertise it quite as loudly. With the top pairing of Nicklas Lidstrom and Larry Murphy in major smother mode (call 'em the Smother Brothers), the Wings held Dallas to 14 shots, four in the final 27 minutes.

"We ran into a team that was a bit rusty, and they played a bit into our hands," Murphy said. "We played real responsibly. That's what it takes."

The Wings know what it takes, especially on the road, where they're an astonishing 6—1 in these playoffs. The Stars are learning what it takes, and the lesson just got accelerated.

Maybe they figured they could dull the Wings to death. Or maybe they hoped the Wings would put the puck in the net for them. Whatever they were thinking, they better think again, because the sellout crowd of 16,928 spent its few wakeful moments Sunday booing a horrid power play and wondering if anyone besides Mike Modano can skate and carry the puck at the same time.

"They don't give you an inch," said Modano, the smooth center from Westland, who stood at his locker looking more dazed than confused. "They backcheck well, they forecheck well, they always seem to have three or four guys on the blue line. I don't think there's much we can change. We just have to play harder."

This was stifling hockey, Wings style. To be honest, I don't know if the Wings completely suffocated Dallas or if the Stars put pillows over their own faces.

Nobody took risks, and after a first period about as exciting as World Cup soccer without the rioting, the Wings stopped waiting for their chances and started creating them.

Slava Kozlov scored on a rebound on a power play, after Lidstrom scrapped to keep the puck in the zone.

Later in the second period, Martin Lapointe, Mr. May, knocked a Star out of the way, took a pass from Jamie Macoun and slid it past Eddie Belfour, who came in as the hottest goalie in the game and left considerably cooler.

At the other end, Chris Osgood wasn't spectacular because the Stars politely declined to force him. He was solid, and when the Wings

If they continue to play this way, the end for the Stars will come quickly. If both teams continue to play this bland style, nobody will be watching on Fox, but that's OK. The Wings stopped worrying a while ago about entertaining, and now concentrate on the finer points of hockey.

For instance, I'm guessing Modano woke up about 3:30 this morning, soaked in sweat, with the scent of Murphy, Lidstrom, Macoun and Bob Rouse still on him. When they weren't harassing Modano, Steve Yzerman and Sergei Fedorov took their turns. More important, once they got the lead, the Wings quelled the urge to relax, and continued to dominate in the third period.

"We have a lot of players who have played a lot of important games on the road," Yzerman said. "We feel comfortable. The key is to not press and not force anything."

Those are the words that make Coach Scotty Bowman beam about this team. Those are the words that must make Dallas Coach Ken Hitchcock cringe.

If the Wings won't force anything, the Stars might have to, and they aren't equipped to do it. Since losing leading scorer Joe Nieuwendyk to a knee injury, they've tried to turtle their way through the playoffs, safe in a shell. They've scored 25 goals in 12 games, and twice went to overtime 0-0.

One game rarely settles a series, and Dallas' big defense still can exact a toll. Playoff hockey can turn suddenly, as the Wings know well. But the omen here was obvious: The Wings played the way the Stars love to play, and beat 'em soundly.

"I don't think they have to open it up, that's not their game," said Wings forward Brent Gilchrist, a former Star. "They'll be real stingy defensively again. But I think these teams are a lot more alike than people depicted."

In other words, if the Stars want to dull it down with numbing defense, fine with the Wings. They know the game, any time, any place.

Wings defenseman Larry Murphy slammed Darryl Sydor into the boards while Sergei Fedorov swooped in to pick up the loose puck.

are playing like this, that's all they request.

"Definitely, by far, our best game defensively," Osgood said. "We really tightened up, took guys away from the middle and moved guys from the front of the net. We're playing so confident right now, almost as if each and every game, we know we'll be there at the end."

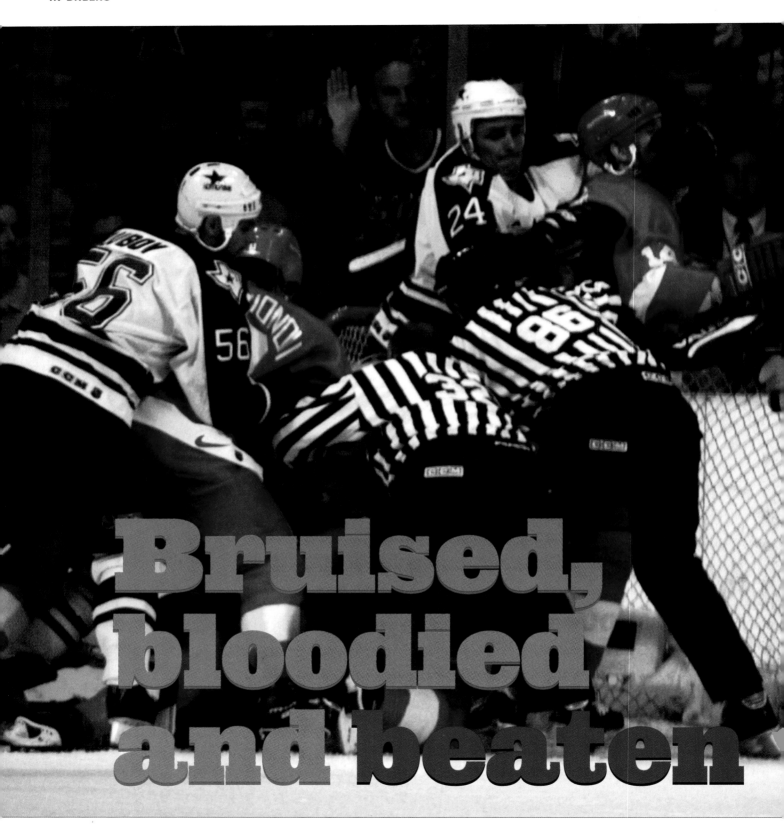

Bruised, bloodied and beaten

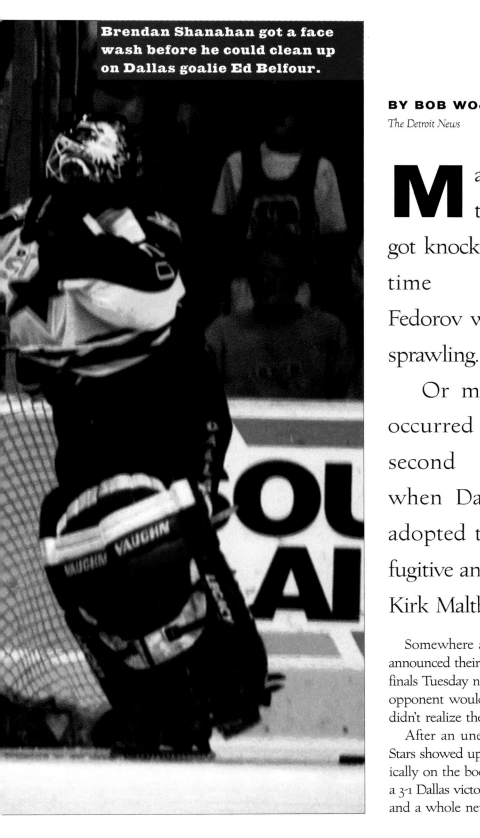

Brendan Shanahan got a face wash before he could clean up on Dallas goalie Ed Belfour.

BY BOB WOJNOWSKI

The Detroit News

Maybe it was the 18th time Steve Yzerman got knocked down or the 15th time Sergei Fedorov was sent sprawling.

Or maybe it occurred in the second period, when Dallas' Craig Ludwig adopted the crazed look of a fugitive and attempted to choke Kirk Maltby.

STARS	WINGS
1	0
1	1
1	0
3	**1**

Somewhere amid all of that, the Dallas Stars announced their arrival in the Western Conference finals Tuesday night. The Red Wings figured their opponent would appear soon enough. They just didn't realize they'd be in such a nasty mood.

After an unexplained one-game absence, the Stars showed up eager to leave their marks, specifically on the bodies of the Wings. The result was a 3-1 Dallas victory, a series tied at one victory each and a whole new pot of gurgling emotion.

"They played tough, they played hard, they kept forechecking," forward Darren McCarty said. "When we sit back and don't use our speed, we're going to lose. We'll go home now, and you better believe we'll be ready."

The Stars saw red, and they hit it. The Wings saw stars, and eventually hit back. Richard Matvichuk and Derian Hatcher, Dallas' big defensemen, went Red-hunting. And every Star, including edgy goalie Eddie Belfour, took a whack at Tomas Holmstrom, who takes a beating and keeps on competing.

The Stars were awful in Game 1, but they came out in Game 2 like caffeine freaks wired on cof-fee. Yzerman and Fedorov were the primary targets, feeling Dallas flesh almost every time they touched the puck.

"I got knocked down a lot, but there's not much I can do, except roll with it," Yzerman said. "They had a lot more energy. But we can play better."

The Wings can take a hit, no doubt. And it became apparent they'd have to deliver a few. They weren't unwitting victims, not with Chris Osgood dumping Pat Verbeek and Mike Modano, not with Martin Lapointe lifting Brian Skrudland by the leg and dropping him, as if executing a wrestling move. Brendan Shanahan even exchanged facial massages with Belfour. Suddenly, it was Duking Night in

Tomas Holmstrom, who was a major headache for the Stars, got his head examined by Sergei Zubov.

Big D, and the crowd loved it.

Ludwig temporarily lost his mind, attacking Maltby with punches to the head, followed by a gentle squeezing of the throat. But the Wings squandered the subsequent four-minute power play, cut a minute short by an Yzerman slash.

"It'll probably get even nastier," Ludwig said, knowing this is how it was expected to be, which isn't necessarily what the Wings wanted. Everyone knows the key to these playoff scrums is composure. The Wings have it, and the Stars tested it. The Stars seemed intent on unnerving them, and Bob Bassen's goal 5:56 into the game presented the opportunity. When Greg Adams made it 2-0, you could hear the grinding sounds of a series forming.

This is where you weather or wither, and the Wings did a decent job weathering. The Stars don't mind taking penalties, and the Wings did have six power plays, without success. They'll need more bodies in front of Belfour and more skating through the neutral zone, but that's not a shocking revelation.

This was a tough, dangerous team announcing it won't go easily. The Wings got the message, along with a few welts. It was more an enlightening show by the Stars than a poor showing by the Wings. It was playoff hockey as we remembered it, and now it's the Wings' turn to bounce back.

Slava Fetisov was sandwiched between Guy Carbonneau (21) and Shawn Chambers.

It was no stretch to say Stars goalie Ed Belfour played well. He made 27 saves in Game 2.

OPPOSITE, RIGHT AND LEFT: JACK GRUBER

STANLEY CUP ROUND 3

GAME 3 MAY 29, 1998

IN DETROIT

Scared straight

Red Wings worried after squandering big lead

BY KEN KLAVON
The Detroit News

WINGS	STARS
2	0
2	1
1	2
5	3

Excuse the Red Wings if they weren't exactly whooping it up after their Game 2 victory.

After playing two periods of determined hockey, the Wings withstood a late scare and defeated the Dallas Stars, 5-3, in Game 3 of the Western Conference finals.

The Wings took a two-games-to-one lead in the best-of-seven series.

Nicklas Lidstrom led the charge with two goals and an assist. Brent Gilchrist, Jamie Macoun and Martin Lapointe also scored for the Wings. Dallas got its offense from Jere Lehtinen (two goals) and Westland native Mike Modano.

"We played a porous game in the third (period)," Wings Coach Scotty Bowman said. "You get caught up watching the scoreboard. We dodged a bullet tonight."

By the first five minutes of the second period, the Wings had a 4-0 lead. But with less than three minutes to play in the game the Wings were fending off an inspired Stars team that cut the lead to 4-3.

"If we had a start like we had finished, I think

OPPOSITE PAGE: DANIEL MEARS

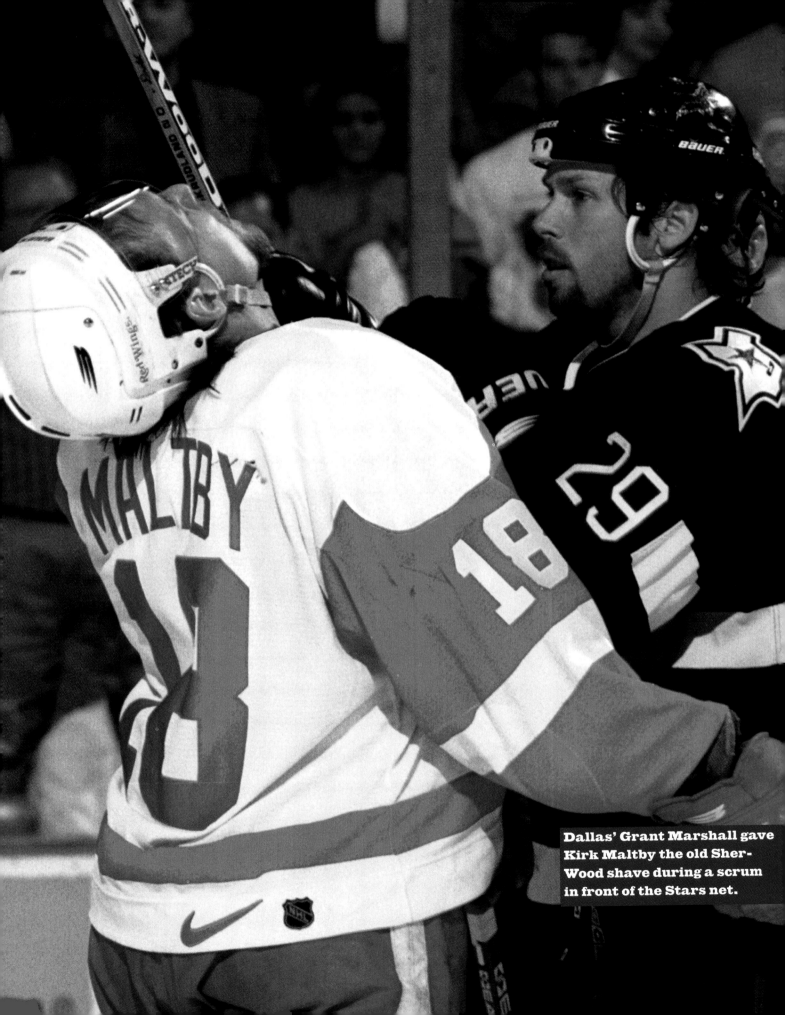

Dallas' Grant Marshall gave Kirk Maltby the old Sher-Wood shave during a scrum in front of the Stars net.

Martin Lapointe iced the game when he scored after Ed Belfour took a dive to try to draw a penalty.

we would be in good shape," Modano said.

"I think we got lucky tonight," Lapointe said. "We let them back in the game. We're not a team that usually does that."

Lucky or not, the Wings came out more aggressive than in Game 2 and forced early errors. It was the first time in 10 games that the Stars gave up more than two goals.

"We haven't played that way in a bit where we made so many mental mistakes," Stars defenseman Darryl Sydor said.

The Stars carried the play most of the period, outshooting the Wings 13-7. But Chris Osgood, who faced 34 shots in all, made several excellent stops. "This might have been the best game he's played," Bowman said.

Seconds after their first of 20 shots on Dallas goalie Ed Belfour, the Wings took advantage of a three-on-two at the 5:50 mark. Steve Yzerman led the break before dishing a pass to Gilchrist, who buried it past Belfour on the short side.

"I just heard him yell and threw the puck there," Yzerman said. "I was actually surprised it got to him."

Moments after the goal, the Wings found themselves on the wrong end of a five-on-three power play for 1:34. But Osgood and the penalty-killing unit was strong, bringing the Joe Louis Arena crowd to its feet as time expired on both penalties.

At 12:43 Lidstrom scored his fourth playoff goal on the power play, and the Wings took a 2-0 lead into the first intermission.

Five minutes into the second the score read 4-0 when Lidstrom and Macoun scored on blasts from the point.

"We always think about the first goal being so important," Bowman said. "We got the first four. ... I think after the second one it stunned them a little bit."

Stunned or not, the Stars appeared to be left to stargaze with more than half the game to play.

At that point, upset with what Dallas players referred to as "too many breakdowns," Coach Ken Hitchcock called a time-out amid the hysteria.

What did he tell them?

"Actually, it was pretty loud," Dallas' Jamie Langenbrunner said. "It was tough to hear him down there. He was saying just to get our game going. We were sitting back and they were taking it to us. We had to start matching their intensity.

"When they came out and scored those goals, we had to step forward and match it."

Whether it was a case of matching intensity or the Wings conveniently punching up cruise control, the Stars managed to make it interesting.

Lehtinen capitalized off a Wings turnover to get the Stars' first goal. Then in the third period Lehtinen scored again and Modano got his first goal in eight games to cut the deficit to 4-3 with 12:27 left.

By that time the Stars had the Wings on their heels.

"When you're not creating chances yourself, you're kind of hanging on, and we did get lucky in the third," Yzerman said.

Perhaps the most critical play of the game occurred when the Wings needed a spark the most.

With less than four minutes to go, Lapointe steamed after a dump-in that Belfour came out to play. Lapointe chopped at Belfour's stick, and Belfour proceeded to flop, looking for a penalty. But referee Terry Gregson shook his head while Belfour stumbled back to the net. Belfour couldn't get set, and Lapointe put in Vyacheslav Kozlov's bank shot between Belfour's legs.

"Kozzie just slapped at it," Lapointe said. "You never know what's going to happen. He knew the goalie wasn't in the net and tried to score."

If anything, the Stars plan on using the third period as motivation for Game 4.

"When we did make mistakes they ended up in our net," Modano said. "We didn't spend a whole lot of time in our zone througout the whole game.

"As the game went on and as the heat turned up, we had to respond; we had to do something.

"If you want to take something positive out of the game, something to build on for (Game 4), it was that we were real loose going into the third. I think it was good that we scored some goals."

Konstantinov's brief visit great for morale

By BOB WOJNOWSKI

The Detroit News

It was the smile they wanted to see, the one he flashed for the cameras 10 minutes earlier, the one he showed infrequently in his days as the NHL's most feared defenseman, the one that has become his most visible sign of communication.

Now, in the dressing room, sitting near his untouched locker, Vlady was back, and so was the smile. Players approached him like a friend who had been away too long. They high-fived. They leaned down to hug him. They kissed him on the cheek. And Vladimir Konstantinov, away too long but not forever, smiled and answered, one by one, haltingly remembering every nickname.

"Hi, Ozzie."

"Hi, Kozzie."

"Hi, Shanny."

"Hi, Mac."

"Hi, Drapes."

Vlady came home Saturday, and for the Red Wings teammates who greeted him, it was all good now, nearly a year after the horrible sadness, after the limousine accident that damaged his brain, ended his hockey career and left him in a wheelchair. It had been three months since they'd seen him in Florida, and they marveled at his progress. His 40-minute visit to the dressing room was respectfully private, and those who were there emerged with emotions churning.

"We were so glad to see him, everyone ran up to him like when you want to see a newborn," Kirk Maltby said. "It was great for morale. He just seemed so happy."

Slowly, the ache fades, replaced by inspiration and images that will never wane. For today's Game 4 of the Western Conference finals against the Dallas Stars, Konstantinov is expected to sit in the owner's suite, and when his face is flashed on the scoreboard, the noise from the crowd will shake loose all the memories — and more than a few tears. The Wings might even consider showing the old "Vladinator" video, highlight clips of his greatest hits. Those who know him best say he seems cheered, not depressed, by images of what used to be.

"He understands everything, he just can't express himself," said Irina Konstantinov, his wife. "He remembers the Stanley Cup, but not all the details of every day of the celebration, which is very sad. He has trouble with short-term memory. Probably a few days after this, he won't remember he was here."

Her eyes watered as she talked about the outpouring from the public, and about a life changed forever.

"He's very excited, very happy to be back," she said. "Doctors say an injury like this can change a person's habits and nature, but I think Vlady's himself. It's him."

This story doesn't have to stay so painful, not when hopeful will work. Konstantinov has made steady progress since the accident June 13, six days after the Wings won the Stanley Cup. He has difficulty talking and didn't speak during a 10-minute news conference Saturday. When he does talk, it's usually in Russian, although he greeted his teammates in English. He can walk with assistance, and rides in the front passenger seat of a

Vladimir Konstantinov and his wife, Irina, waved to friends in the crowd during a news conference to mark his return to Joe Louis Arena.

standard Mercedes sedan, not a specially equipped van.

He often tells Irina he will play again, that he'll start practicing next month. In Florida, he sat in his driveway and swung a stick at tennis balls tossed by his daughter, Anastasia. He had longed for the familiarity of the game and the team he loves, and on the flight up, he was so excited, he couldn't sleep. On Saturday at Joe Louis Arena, he wore a white Hockeytown sweatshirt and black sweatpants, and when trainer John Wharton and two security guards lifted him in his wheelchair to the podium, he flashed the smile, and waved his left hand.

The heartache never totally ends, not for Irina and Anastasia, not for teammates who remember his incomparable blend of talent and toughness, not for fans who lined up at Metro Airport on Friday and gave Vlady a standing ovation. It doesn't end, but it doesn't hurt as much as it used to. This is more about remembering than despairing.

"It's been loud in the Joe before, but it'll be nothing compared to when they introduce Vlady," Kris Draper said. "The one thing we don't want to do, when he sees us play, is let him down. We haven't gotten over losing him, but it's healthy medicine for him and for us to see him again. His spirit is what pushes us."

It has pushed them since training camp, when players knew they'd have to fill the toughness void. It pushes them every time they see his locker.

"He's still part of the team and we're thrilled to see him," captain Steve Yzerman said. "You can only feel bad for so long, and you have to move on. I never got the sense Vlady felt sorry for himself."

There are some who will wonder how Konstantinov's presence will affect the Wings today, but really, it's trite to wonder. The Wings likely will play as Konstantinov played, with unchecked passion. Of greater importance is the benefit to Konstantinov, who seems capable of sitting in a familiar place, in front of his locker with the skates and pads and stone engraved with "Believe," and remembering how everything used to be.

He is reminded constantly, in the 50 boxes of letters he has received. He is reminded by teammates who joke about the return of the blond streaks, the old Vladinator hairstyle.

"The instant you see him, it's like he never left," Wharton said. "I think everyone on the team just wants to get to a point where they can hang out with him. This is who he is now, but you can't avoid who he was. To be honest, I miss the ornery Vlady, the one who drove me crazy."

Wharton smiled, reflecting the mood of the day. A few feet away, Irina helped Vlady into the car, and as she dismantled the wheelchair and placed it in the trunk, he sat in the front seat and reached for the window visor. He looked in the mirror and adjusted his cap, and suddenly, there it was again, the smile that let's us know it's not all sad anymore. The Vladinator might never return, but Vlady's back.

TODD McINTURF

Kirk Maltby's shorthanded
goal gave the Wings the
early lead again.

Wings win, Stars dim

BY CYNTHIA LAMBERT
The Detroit News

These Red Wings know how to let suspense build. Vladimir Konstantinov and Sergei Mnatsakanov sat in owner Mike Ilitch's box at Joe Louis Arena for Game 4,

WINGS	STARS
2	1
1	0
0	1
3	**2**

and the Red Wings gave tnem an eyeful in a tense and sometimes sloppy 3-2 victory over the Stars.

DANIEL MEARS

97

Tomas Holmstrom countered Brian Skrudland's stick between the legs by pulling Skrudland's sweater.

JACK GRUBER

The Wings lead the Western Conference finals three games to one. They can reach the Stanley Cup Finals for the third time in four years with a victory in Game 5 at Dallas.

"Sometimes it's not pretty, but the bottom line is to win," forward Darren McCarty said.

The Wings led 2-0 after the first period on goals by Kirk Maltby (shorthanded) and Steve Yzerman (power play). But the Stars got back into the game, and the score was 2-2 after Sergei Zubov got a power-play goal 55 seconds into the third period. Pat Verbeek scored for the Stars late in the second.

The Wings made it 3-2 when Vyacheslav Kozlov deflected Larry Murphy's shot past Ed Belfour at 11:30 of the third for his fourth winning goal of the playoffs.

"We took the lead again and seemed to have trouble in the second period," Coach Scotty Bowman said. "We had our best period in the third. It was one of those games where you knew the next goal was going to win it. But the ice was pretty tough on both teams. I've never seen the puck bounce like that. ... The puck was bouncing like a ball."

Bowman blamed the puck used for Fox television broadcasts. The puck has a computer chip inside and it can't be frozen. Perhaps Bowman wanted the focus taken off his team's inability to hold a lead. In Game 3, the Wings led 4-0 before winning 5-3.

"They're a team that's not going to go away," Yzerman said of the Stars.

One more loss and the Stars will be history. The Wings have three chances to clinch the series, but they don't want to get caught looking ahead.

"We've made that mistake before ...," goalie Chris Osgood said. "We did that against New Jersey in the Finals (in 1995). This has been a very close series. Any of the games could have gone either way."

Breaks bounce Red Wings' way, but, hey, they were due a few

By BOB WOJNOWSKI

The Detroit News

No team knows the peculiar nature of fate like the Red Wings. No team knows how suddenly things can turn, how crazily the puck can bounce.

In another odd game in a weird series, on a day when they were reminded how fortune, good and bad, can visit at the strangest times, the Wings went ahead and took a game they had to have. They didn't outplay, outhit or outshoot Dallas, but maybe the Wings are owed a few breaks.

High above the ice in the owner's luxury box Sunday, Vladimir Konstantinov and Sergei Mnatsakanov watched for the first time since both suffered severe head injuries in the limo accident last June 13, six days after Detroit won the Stanley Cup. What they saw was a team take its most important step — unsteady but so determined — toward defending its title. The Wings held off the charging Stars 3-2 to grab a 3-1 lead in the series, one victory from the finals.

Who knows for sure what's pushing them now, because they're not finding much separation from the Stars. The Wings didn't overuse the presence of their injured friends as motivation, honoring them respectfully midway through the first period, when their pictures were shown on the scoreboard screen.

The crowd stood and cheered for nearly two minutes, as players on both teams tapped their sticks on the ice. On the Detroit bench, eyes welled. One player who fought back tears was Slava Kozlov, Konstantinov's Russian buddy, and with the game tied in the third period, it was Kozlov who reached out to deflect the puck past Ed Belfour for the winning goal.

In the dressing room afterward, Mnatsakanov congratulated Kozlov, the quiet little winger who always seems to score the biggest goals.

"He was very happy, and I am too," Kozlov said. "I appreciate all the people who cheered and remembered Sergei and Vlady. As for my goal, everybody pays attention to the big players and sometimes they forget about me. I'm just standing in the right spot."

The Wings stand in this spot for many reasons — because captain Steve Yzerman was brilliant again, scoring one goal and setting up Kozlov's; because goalie Chris Osgood is making his detractors look silly, outplaying Belfour, just as he outplayed Grant Fuhr in the previous series.

But the main reason they're one step from the Finals is they don't often forget how they got there.

They aren't here by happenstance, fueled by some sudden burst of emotion. They're here because they're seizing opportunity, and for all its tenacity, Dallas keeps presenting chances.

Kirk Maltby picked up a turnover by Richard Matvichuk and skated in alone for the game's first goal. Yzerman, who has been relentless, jabbed in his own rebound on a power play for a 2-0 lead.

The Stars fought back on goals by Pat Verbeek and Sergei Zubov, who snapped Dallas' ridiculous 1-for-52 power-play drought. But in a wild final 30 seconds, Osgood slid left and right, amid sticks and falling bodies, then made the clinching save on a Zubov sizzler with 6.5 seconds left.

Dallas Coach Ken Hitchcock said Osgood is playing as well as he's ever seen. The Wings are hardly surprised.

"It's you guys (in the media) who always make a big deal out of it," Darren McCarty said. "Ozzie's a great goalie. People should just get off his back. He's mentally tough and he always bounces back."

Osgood keeps proving it, whether his critics notice or not. The Wings desperately needed him because Dallas outshot them again, 30-23. That's 64 shots by the Stars in two games, in which the Wings have frittered away leads.

That's a concern, and Game 5 in Dallas will be a difficult close-out. The Wings, who always regain composure, are playing a bit haughty, the Stars a bit naughty. Sergei Fedorov and Brendan Shanahan — each without a goal in the series — still must make an impact, and as long as Belfour is acting goofy, they have a shot.

With Detroit already on a power play in the second period, Belfour attempted to clear Martin Lapointe from the net by forcefully jabbing his stick between Lapointe's legs. The penalty gave the Wings a two-man advantage, and shortly after, Yzerman scored.

"He didn't get me in the right spot, or it could have been serious," Lapointe said with a shrug. "When somebody does that, you want to make them pay. ... They're a good team. They won't let up. We have to be careful."

This time of year, everybody does what they can. Up in the suite, Konstantinov and Mnatsakanov responded to the crowd by waving white pom pons, Vlady with his good left hand, Sergei with his good right hand. During the ovation, a warm display that heeded the Wings' desire to avoid being maudlin, Mnatsakanov wept.

It was a day of emotions, raw and real, a day to be reminded about the short distance from euphoria to tragedy, from winning to losing. It's a gap the Wings know better than anyone.

Vyacheslav Kozlov tipped the puck past a startled Ed Belfour in the third period of Game 4. It was Kozlov's fourth game-winner of the playoffs.

Osgood's blunder gives Dallas thunder

BY BOB WOJNOWSKI

The Detroit News

The puck came from center ice, fired nearly 90 feet, and by the time it arrived at Chris Osgood's stick, it had the momentum to wound. Osgood reached for it and missed, and

STARS	WINGS
1	1
1	1
0	0
1	0
3	**2**

Not again: Jamie Langenbrunner's 88-foot dagger found the
net but not Chris Osgood's heart.

DANIEL MEARS

now, we'll learn exactly how tough he is, and how badly the Wings were hurt.

Osgood muffed the shot by Jamie Langenbrunner 46 seconds into overtime, a stunning gaffe that sent the shellshocked goalie to the bench and the Wings home with a 3-2 loss Wednesday night. Detroit still clings to a three-games-to-two lead in the Western Conference finals, but this will be the ultimate test, especially for the young Osgood, who surrendered a similar goal to St. Louis in the previous round.

The linesmen jumped into a pile of Wings and Stars to break up a scrum near the Dallas goal in Game 5.

How could it happen again? There can be no plausible explanation, and no excuses. More important, how quickly can Osgood and the Wings recover? This was a game they had, but Dallas tied it with 1:25 left in regulation, then won it on the shot heard all across Texas.

The play looked innocent enough, with Langenbrunner crossing the red line before letting it go. Osgood skated out of the crease and tried to stop it with his stick. That quickly, he became the focal point of the series, the pressure shifting suddenly from Dallas' unsteady Ed Belfour to Osgood.

Osgood was on the team bus quickly, headed home to a Joe Louis Arena crowd that can be unforgiving. Right now, forgiving isn't what concerns the Wings. Forgetting is the first step.

"There's nothing we can do about that game now," captain Steve Yzerman said. "It doesn't matter how they won it. We don't need to say anything to (Osgood). He's not happy about it. He's a tough, cocky kid. He doesn't need any pats on the back when he does well or when he doesn't."

Osgood has shown his toughness before, when he surrendered a center-ice goal to St. Louis' Al MacInnis, tying that game in the final minute. Osgood was excellent in overtime and the Wings won, 3-2.

This will be more difficult, because once is a fluke, twice is a problem. Osgood had cooled his critics with several fine games, but now he's back under the hot lights. Nothing is as devastating as being on the verge of vanquishing a foe, then letting them up.

"We talked about throwing the puck at (Osgood), low and hard," Dallas' Mike Modano said. "As the game went on, you could see him second-guessing himself. But he's always come back and had strong games, so I don't think we can count him out."

The desperate die hard, something the Wings learned on a sweltering night. The Stars, staring down elimination, would not go quietly, pestering and pressing the Wings. If the Wings were to reach their third Stanley Cup final in four years, they'd have to do it the hard way.

The Stars' Guy Carbonneau tied the game 2-2 with 1:25 left in regulation, digging the puck out of the corner, getting knocked down, then hopping up to fire a shot that ticked Nicklas Lidstrom's stick and sailed over Osgood's left shoulder. The deflection affected Osgood, but if he makes that save, the Wings are home, getting ready for the Finals.

Frankly, the Stars earned another chance, because no matter how many times the Wings put 'em in a hole, they popped out. The Wings tried to milk Igor Larionov's second-period goal, lapsing into a defensive shell, and it failed. Dallas stayed dangerous, and when Carbonneau's shot slipped past, everything turned.

This was classic playoff hockey, all persistence and emotion. But the Wings have had a horrible tendency to sit back with a lead, and it cost them.

"Dallas obviously isn't giving up," Yzerman said. "But we've been in this situation a few times. It happens. I don't see it as bouncing back. It's just moving on."

If the Wings are to move on, they'll have to earn it. Scotty Bowman called Dallas the toughest opponent since the Wings were swept in the 1995 finals by New Jersey. The Stars' defense afforded little breathing room, and they came out as if they weren't ready for the off-season, forcing Osgood to make several fine saves. It has been the pattern of the series, with the Stars taking more shots and delivering more hits, and the Wings waiting ... waiting for their opportunity.

They got goals from Tomas Holmstrom and Larionov, then tried to hang on. They had their chances, with Yzerman and Brendan Shanahan getting stopped point-blank, and Lidstrom hitting a post.

Osgood's flub is the headline, naturally, but the Wings were badly outshot again, 36-20. Still, they fell only 90 seconds and 90 feet short. The last goal is one Osgood simply cannot allow, but he did, and the pressure is on him to rebound.

The Wings have faced adversity before, but this is big. With one shot, the Stars got life, and Osgood got more unwanted attention. As always, the key is the response, and when the teams meet in Game 6, it should be interesting. Osgood gets another chance, and he and the Wings had better not waste this one.

Dallas' Jamie Langenbrunner raised his stick in celebration after his 88-foot shot stunned the Red Wings and gave the Stars new life.

Sergei Fedorov's goal was the final margin of victory. His inspired play helped put the Wings in the Finals.

Ozzie spells doom for Dallas

Wings goalie answers critics with shutout

BY DAVE DYE
The Detroit News

The term "day-to-day" in sports usually refers to the status of an injured player. With Red Wings goalie Chris Osgood, it also describes Hockeytown's love-hate relationship with him.

WINGS	STARS
1	0
1	0
0	0
2	0

Nicklas Lidstrom and Larry Murphy mobbed goalie Chris Osgood after the Wings eliminated Dallas behind Osgood's rock-solid play.

ALAN LESSIG

Igor Larionov hooked down Mike Keane as Dallas ended the series the way it began — losing 2-0.

The Western Conference final started 13 days ago with a shutout by Osgood and it ended in Game 6 with another shutout by him.

But in between, some people wanted to run him out of town.

If Osgood goes, he might just take the Stanley Cup with him.

The defending champs are returning to the Stanley Cup Finals for the third time in four years.

They won the West with a 2-0 victory over the Dallas Stars at Joe Louis Arena to clinch the series, four games to two.

Some still will say the Wings are going back in spite of Osgood. They could be right in a way. Lesser teams wouldn't have overcome the two crucial goals on shots from center ice allowed by Osgood in the last two rounds.

Teams with less character wouldn't have come

back to beat St. Louis in overtime the first time it happened. And they wouldn't have been able to rebound the second time — an overtime loss in Game 5 at Dallas — to finish off a team two days later that had the league's best regular-season record.

But, like his entire team, Osgood again showed he can handle adversity with the best. Now, if he can just handle a 90-foot shot by Joe Juneau.

"When we have a little adversity, it seems to spur us on," Wings Coach Scotty Bowman said. "We had our best game of the series."

V for victory: Chris Osgood's perfect performance in Game 6 exorcised the ghost of Jamie Langenbrunner's 88-foot overtime goal.

If the Wings can overcome the tragic loss of Vladimir Konstantinov, they can overcome a few fluke goals.

But Wings fans knew their team needed to win Game 6 or the chance of back-to-back titles would be greatly diminished. So, they got behind their goalie before the game started, chanting "Oz-zie. Oz-zie."

"The fans were echoing our sentiments," said Wings defenseman Larry Murphy, whose short-handed goal gave the Wings a 1-0 lead at 6:20 of the first period. "He was the best goalie in the series."

"We knew he'd be our best player tonight," defenseman Bob Rouse said of Osgood.

Shortly after the Wings took a 2-0 lead, Osgood was tested three times in less than a minute. Mike Keane failed to lift the puck when he was on the doorstep and had Osgood out of position. Moments later, Mike Modano was stopped twice in 10 seconds, once from the high slot and once from the low slot.

This was Osgood's night, the Wings' night. He made 26 saves for his fifth career playoff shutout.

The 88-foot winning shot in Game 5 by the Stars' Jamie Langenbrunner isn't forgotten, but it is forgiven. It didn't cost the Wings a chance for the Cup as many feared it might.

"It was satisfying," Osgood said of his shutout. "I've been beat twice from the red line. But who cares now? I'm not going to let two plays put a mark on what I'm doing. It's ridiculous."

The response by the crowd was special for Osgood. They really want to love him, not hate him.

Said Osgood: "It felt real good to have the fans behind me. That meant more to me than anything that's happened here besides winning the Stanley Cup. It made me feel comfortable and made it easier to play."

The Wings advance to face the surging Washington Capitals. At least for the moment, Chris

Focused Wings won't celebrate until the job is done

By BOB WOJNOWSKI

The Detroit News

The room was strangely quiet, no blaring music, no shouts, no excited chatter. Players sat at lockers, talking softly. No one wore Western Conference title caps, or T-shirts. The Clarence Campbell Bowl sat atop a water bucket, against the wall, out of the way.

So much accomplished, so much more to go. So much the same, so much different.

The Red Wings have soared back to the Stanley Cup Finals, pushed by experience and poise, pulled by history, stalked but never stopped by adversity. They reached the Finals for the third time in four years with a crunching 2-0 victory over the Dallas Stars on Friday night that was all about business. Celebrate? Not now, not yet. The Washington Capitals are next, Finals neophytes who probably have no idea what they're about to face.

The Wings know. They wear the look of aging warriors who fight on because it's what they do, because as long as fate and foes keep lining up challenges, they might as well keep knocking them down.

This has been the most taxing road, six brutal games to beat Dallas, six games to eliminate both St. Louis and Phoenix. It's even tougher if you go back to where it started, last June 13, six days after winning the city's first Stanley Cup in 42 years, the day star defenseman Vladimir Konstantinov and trainer Sergei Mnatsakanov were struck with horrible injuries in a limo crash. (Defenseman Slava Fetisov was also injured in the accident but

recovered to continue playing at the age of 40).

Then, just before the season, General Manager Ken Holland made the bold decision to trade playoff MVP Mike Vernon and give young Chris Osgood a shot in net. Later, Sergei Fedorov's contract dispute boiled over.

From there to here, back at the lip of the Cup, was the longest, toughest route, and the Wings just lowered their heads and trudged forward, because it's what they do.

"Vlady and Vernie (his absence) is definitely part of the motivation," captain Steve Yzerman said. "Our team is trying to prove something. Ozzie is trying to prove something. Being Stanley Cup champion was a great experience, a great memory, but it's gone."

Somehow, in this era of pro athletes growing content, this team found new challenges, while searching for a memory to erase last summer's aborted celebration. You could see it in training camp, when players resolved to fill the holes left by Konstantinov and Vernon. Go back to the pre-season publications and try to find anyone picking the Wings to repeat.

So they didn't return to the Finals because they were supposed to. They returned because they didn't lose their way. Sixteen different Wings have scored in these playoffs, as they still blend stars and grinders, offense and defense, grace and grit, better than any team in the league.

"In some ways, things came easily to us last year," Brendan Shanahan said. "We've had to work for everything this year. We've had a lot thrown at us

The Clarence Campbell Bowl sat unnoticed atop a water bucket in the Wings locker room after Game 6.

and we just ignored it and played harder. We've had muckers play like stars and stars play like muckers."

Give credit to the coach, Scotty Bowman, the best ever, for allowing players to break through barriers, for letting grinders such as Martin Lapointe and Tomas Holmstrom expand and explore their goal-scoring ability.

Give credit to Yzerman for not resting with the ultimate accomplishment, for being driven enough to want more.

Give credit to Fedorov, who returned to high-flying form, leading everyone with nine goals.

Goodness, give credit to Osgood, who merely played brilliantly through all the doubts. We've been saying for months this 25-year-old is stronger than you know, and if you need more proof, well, wait a couple of weeks, he'll be happy to provide it.

"It's very satisfying," Osgood said. "I don't care anymore what people say. I feel great out there, and I'm just going to play."

The formula hasn't really changed. Without Konstantinov, the defense isn't quite as tight, but with steady Nicklas Lidstrom and veterans Lar-

ry Murphy and Bob Rouse, it's savvy. Winning can be addictive, and the Wings are hooked. No NHL team has repeated since Pittsburgh in 1991-92. No champion even returned to the Finals the year after, not until now.

The Wings chew adversity like energy bars. Osgood has surrendered four soft goals, and won the next game each time. During the past two postseasons, the Wings are 9-1 following a loss.

The Capitals have experience, if not Finals experience, and they'll be ready. They might even think the Wings are weary, prime to be plucked. My guess is they will be mistaken.

"We're not taking anything for granted," Yzerman said, in the still of the dressing room. "All the experiences we've had — good and bad — have helped us. We feel comfortable in tight games and difficult situations."

You prove it once, you want to prove it again. For all they've been through, the Wings haven't lost the look, the one Dallas just witnessed, the one Washington is about to see. The job isn't done, the challenge isn't over. For these Wings, it never is.

DANIEL MEARS

Wings vs. Capitals

**Tomas Holmstrom
celebrates Nicklas
Lidstrom's goal.**

Wings slay Caps' Godzilla

Kolzig fooled by consecutive shots in first period

BY CYNTHIA LAMBERT

The Detroit News

O ne of the Red Wings' biggest concerns entering Game 1 of the Stanley Cup Finals was Olaf Kolzig, who has a reputation as large as his 6-foot-3, 225-pound frame and a nickname of Godzilla to match.

But on consecutive shots midway through the first period, the Wings exposed Kolzig for what he really is — a man wearing goalie equipment. And at the end of Game 1, the Wings owned a 2-1 victory.

"He looks big in the net," defenseman Nicklas Lidstrom, who scored the Wings' second goal, said of Kolzig.

"When he goes down, he takes away every-

thing on the ice and anything one foot above. What we have to do is screen him, just like Holmer (Tomas Holmstrom) did on my shot. (Kolzig) is so good on his feet and moving side to side."

The Wings outshot the Capitals, 31-17, and most of the Capitals' best chances occurred in the last half of the third period. The Capitals also started stronger than the Wings, but the tide turned after they trailed 2-0.

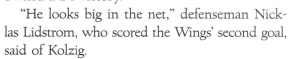

OVERLEAF: DANIEL MEARS; OPPOSITE: DANIEL MEARS

"I thought in the first 10 minutes we played quite well," Capitals Coach Ron Wilson said. "Then our No. 1 and 2 lines got outplayed by their No. 3 and 4 lines. We got a little comfortable — a little lackadaisical."

The Wings took a 1-0 lead when Joe Kocur redirected Doug Brown's centering pass past Kolzig at 14:04 of the first. It was Kocur's fourth goal of the playoffs and the second time in two years he had scored in the Finals opener.

The Wings made it 2-0 when Lidstrom's shot from the left point beat Kolzig cleanly on the stick side at 16:18 of the first. Kocur's and Lidstrom's shots were the Wings' sixth and seven of the game.

On the Capitals' third shot of the second period — and ninth of the game — Richard Zednik scored from above the left hash mark to make it 2-1. The goal ended Chris Osgood's shutout streak at 95 minutes, 57 seconds.

There were tense moments for the Wings in the closing moments after Kolzig was pulled for an extra attacker.

"We seem to be getting used to that the last three or four games," Osgood said. "But we kept them to the outside pretty good. We kept our composure. For the most part, when we got the puck, we were pretty patient."

Joe Kocur raises his hands after giving the Wings a 1-0 lead.

Charting the Red Wings' shots

● Goal   ● Shot   ○ Power-play goal

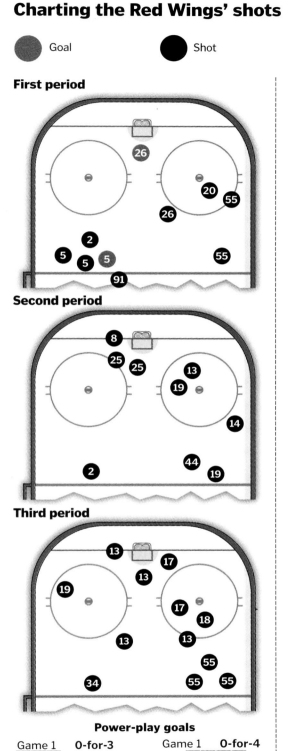

First period

26 · 20 · 55 · 26 · 2 · 5 · 5 · 5 · 55 · 91

Second period

8 · 25 · 25 · 13 · 19 · 14 · 2 · 44 · 19

Third period

13 · 17 · 13 · 19 · 17 · 18 · 13 · 13 · 55 · 34 · 55 · 55

Power-play goals

Game 1   **0-for-3**   Game 1   **0-for-4**

Summaries

No.	Player	Shots
2	FETISOV	2
5	LIDSTROM	3
8	LARIONOV	1
13	KOZLOV	5
14	SHANAHAN	1
17	BROWN	2
18	MALTBY	1
19	YZERMAN	3
20	LAPOINTE	1
25	McCARTY	2
26	KOCUR	2
34	MACOUN	1
44	ERIKSSON	1
55	MURPHY	5
91	FEDOROV	1

Series statistics
(through Game 1)

Shots

Wings   Capitals

31   17

Goals

2   1

Penalties

4   3

Penalty minutes

8   6

Referees
found out
the hard
way that
Wings
Coach
Scotty
Bowman
wasn't
content
with seven
Stanley
Cups.

TOP: DANIEL MEARS; BOTTOM: JACK GRUBER

Vyacheslav
Kozlov
ended up on
the wrong
side of
Godzilla,
Caps goalie
Olaf Kolzig.

TOP: ALAN LESSIG; BOTTOM: DANIEL MEARS

Unsung heroes

Holmstrom finds his comfort zone

BY JOHN NIYO
The Detroit News

He paced and fidgeted and fretted. Finally, Tomas Holmstrom was where he felt comfortable. On the ice, with sticks in his face, cross-checks in his back and pucks whizzing around him.

Welcome to the Stanley Cup Finals, Holmer.

"I wanted to have the game start right away," Holmstrom said after helping the Red Wings to a 2-1 victory in Game 1. "I didn't want to walk around here for two hours waiting for the game. But it's nice to be in the game and to get the win."

And to play.

"It's a big difference," said Holmstrom, a playoff hero this year after missing last year's run to the Stanley Cup. "It's like night and day, really. To be out there is great."

To be out there contributing is even better. Holmstrom assisted on each of the Wings' goals and has six goals and 10 assists in the playoffs. He is fourth on the team in scoring. Not bad for a mucker who had five goals and 22 points in 57 regular-season games.

"Even when you don't play, you learn, but you learn the hard way," said Holmstrom, who can't explain his sudden scoring surge.

"I don't go out there thinking I'm going to put up the points," he said. "I'm just playing my game."

Holmstrom had said he expected to feel the nerves before Game 1. Who could blame him? This scene is new to him and rookie defenseman Anders Eriksson.

"It's not an easy situation for a young player like that," Wings associate coach Dave Lewis said. "Tomas sat and watched all last season. Every day, he wanted to get in the lineup — now he's in the lineup."

And, lo and behold, he's irreplaceable.

Holmstrom drew the second assist on the Wings' first-period goals. But he deserved more credit than that.

On the first goal, he snagged the Capitals' clearing attempt along the boards in the neutral zone and started the play that put the Wings ahead to stay.

"On that first goal, their defense tried to step up and Tomas chipped behind them," said Doug Brown, who centered a line with Holmstrom and Joe Kocur.

Holmstrom, who took a vicious hit on the play, chipped the puck to Brown, who caught a glimpse of Kocur breaking to the net. Brown's backhander found Kocur on the edge of the crease, and Kocur's deflection resulted in the first goal of the Finals.

Holmstrom also had much to do with the Wings' second goal. His work in the corners

After sitting out the 1997 playoffs, Tomas Holmstrom spent most of the 1998 Stanley Cup run fighting off defenders in front of the opposing goalie.

knocked the puck free and out to the point, where Nicklas Lidstrom was waiting to unleash a slap shot. It sailed wide of Holmstrom — positioned in front of goalie Olaf Kolzig — but inside the far post to make it 2-0.

"He plays the same," Lidstrom said of Holmstrom. "It doesn't matter if it's an exhibition game or the regular season or the Stanley Cup Finals. He's the same — always."

Holmstrom's coaches noticed long ago.

"He always brings his competitiveness," Lewis said. "And when a guy does that, good things seem to happen. He just competes so hard for every inch of the ice. What he brings is that hard work, that determination and that relentless, relentless, relentless effort."

That effort was rewarded in a big way Tuesday.

"Tomas had a great game," Brown said. "But we've come to expect that from him."

Capitals introduced to Red Wings hockey

By BOB WOJNOWSKI

The Detroit News

You're a huge favorite. Every neutral observer expects you to win, win big, win quickly. That can be a problem, especially if the underdog catches those whiffs of confidence, just by hanging around.

It can be a problem if you let it, and the Red Wings wouldn't let it, not in Game 1 of the Stanley Cup Finals, not with the ultimate prize growing ever closer. Oh, Washington didn't go away and probably won't go away. But the key, when two unfamiliar foes meet, is that the favorite didn't let one get away.

The Wings' 2-1 victory in Game 1 wasn't scintillating, just stifling in its simplicity. Both teams can play better, we hope, now that they've been duly introduced.

"We had a 2-0 lead and we tried to hang on, and that's disappointing," Darren McCarty said. "We expect more of ourselves. Give Washington credit. They didn't quit, but we've got to skate better. We were fortunate, we know that."

Self-criticism is vital, and certainly, some of it is warranted. The Wings have trouble handling that dreaded two-goal lead, a problem they can't explain and apparently can't solve. But they outshot the Caps, 31-17, and they made a quick impression on goalie Olaf Kolzig.

There was Joe Kocur, Mr. Finals, a man with six goals in the regular season, beating the unbeatable Kolzig in the first period. There was Nicklas Lidstrom, 134 seconds later, dazzling Kolzig on a blue-line slapper. Just like that, the 6-foot-3 goalie they call Godzilla was looking like your basic garden-variety lizard, although not for long.

The Capitals sneaked into these Finals because no one really saw them coming, and no one knew how good Kolzig was. The Wings know now. Fortunately for them, Chris Osgood again met the challenge — the Wizard vs. the Lizard — in a game that was all about introductions.

"I think both teams were looking at each other, trying to figure out what to do," said Sergei Fedorov, who was bottled up most of the night. "We got off to a quick start, then went to sleep. It was a boring game, seems to me."

Seems to me, boredom favors the Capitals. If they're to have a chance, it'll be because of Kolzig, owner of a 1.69 goals-against average in the playoffs, capable of turning shooters to mutterers and an offense to mush. To prevent that, the Wings introduced Mr. "Olie the Goalie" to Mr. "Kocur the Enforcer."

Kocur has been here before, a couple of times. He won a Stanley Cup with the Rangers in 1994. He scored in Game 1 of the 1997 Finals against Philadelphia, launching the Wings' sweep. So if you believe in omens, you got your moment when Kocur took a pass from Doug Brown, who had taken a pass from Tomas Holmstrom, who had scrapped like he always does to get the puck. Kocur guided it into the net as deftly as a fisherman dropping a line, which is what he loves to do in his spare time. He had down time in the previous round, sitting out in favor of Brent Gilchrist, whose groin injury gave Kocur another shot.

"Brownie made a great play; I just did the easy part," Kocur said. "Right place, right time."

You never know when Scotty Bowman will pick the place, or the time. The Brown-Holmstrom-

Kocur trio was a new creation, and it was so successful, Bowman altered it on the next shift. Suddenly, Holmstrom was playing alongside McCarty, and the two were digging the puck, sending it to Lidstrom, who sent it past Kolzig. It was 2-0, and you could see the Capitals cringing, as if they were experiencing something for the first time, which they are.

Washington didn't collect its first shot of the second period until the midway point, and the Wings seemed in total control. But although this is the first Finals appearance in the franchise's 24-year history, the Capitals, 7-1 on the road this postseason, weren't going to crumble (at least not yet). Richard Zednik's goal late in the period gave the Capitals their first breath in a while.

"We don't feel like we were dominated by any stretch of the imagination," Washington Coach Ron Wilson said. "I know we can play better, but Detroit probably can, too."

The Wings can, and they'd better, because as the game progressed, Kolzig regenerated to Godzilla status. The Capitals seemed intent on making some kind of impression, especially on Steve Yzerman, who was kneed by Chris Simon on one play, wrestled to the ice by Dale Hunter on another. Hunter sat on Yzerman for about 30 seconds as the crowd booed. The hope is, there will be less sitting around, now that introductions have been completed.

This was a tough game for the favorite, the opener at home, the one the underdog often steals.

Despite the Caps' lone goal, Chris Osgood answered his critics.

Draper's goal caps comeback

Wings rally from two-goal deficits to win in OT

BY CYNTHIA LAMBERT

The Detroit News

It took 60 shots and nearly four periods for the Red Wings to put the finishing touches on their best and biggest comeback of the playoffs this year.

WINGS				
1	0	3	1	5
1	0	3	0	4
CAPITALS				

Olie the Goalie was magnificent stopped 55 shots, but he could only watch as Kris Draper's feed from Martin Lapointe found the back of the net.

JACK GRUBER

Kris Draper's first goal of the playoffs was a turning point in the series.

Olaf Kolzig made the initial save but couldn't control the rebound, and Steve Yzerman swept in to tuck the puck between the post and Kolzig's pad.

Kris Draper scored 15:24 into overtime to give the Wings a 5-4 victory over the Washington Capitals in Game 2 of the Stanley Cup Finals.

The Wings lead the best-of-seven series, two games to none. Games 3 and 4 are at the MCI Center in Washington.

Only three teams have rallied to win a Finals series after losing the first two games.

"We were on a line change and I didn't think Washington saw me," Draper said. "I put my stick on the ice and Marty (Lapointe) made a great pass to me. I one-timed it into the open net."

The net was open because goalie Olaf Kolzig was concentrating on Brendan Shanahan and Lapointe fighting for the puck with Capitals defenders in the right corner. Draper sprinted from the bench and caught Lapointe's attention.

"I think everybody was tired," Lapointe said. "Shanny did a good job getting me the puck. I saw Kris curling toward the net and I thought, 'This is it.'"

Draper's first goal of the playoffs capped a tremendous comeback by the Wings, who trailed 3-1 and 4-2 in the third period.

Charting the Red Wings' shots

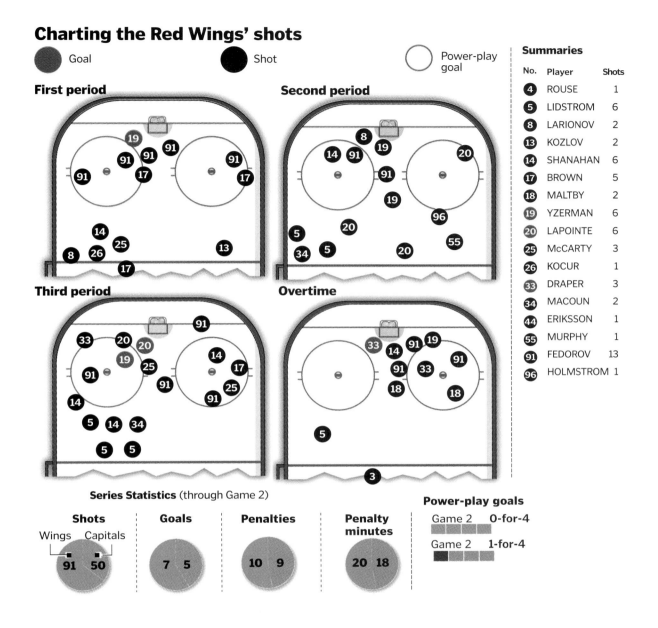

● Goal ● Shot ○ Power-play goal

First period

Second period

Third period

Overtime

Summaries

No.	Player	Shots
4	ROUSE	1
5	LIDSTROM	6
8	LARIONOV	2
13	KOZLOV	2
14	SHANAHAN	6
17	BROWN	5
18	MALTBY	2
19	YZERMAN	6
20	LAPOINTE	6
25	McCARTY	3
26	KOCUR	1
33	DRAPER	3
34	MACOUN	2
44	ERIKSSON	1
55	MURPHY	1
91	FEDOROV	13
96	HOLMSTROM	1

Series Statistics (through Game 2)

Shots
Wings Capitals
91 50

Goals
7 5

Penalties
10 9

Penalty minutes
20 18

Power-play goals

Game 2 0-for-4

Game 2 1-for-4

"It's a great win for us," said Lapointe, who also scored. "There's no doubt, after we tied it, we were feeling pretty confident that we could win if we kept shooting on the net."

The Wings' confidence took a beating in the second period, when their 1-0 lead on a first-period goal by Steve Yzerman was wiped out by three Capitals goals. Peter Bondra (on a play the Wings thought was icing), Chris Simon and Adam Oates scored by 11:03 of the second to give the Capitals a 3-1 lead entering the third.

Yzerman's shorthanded goal at 6:37 of the third sparked the Wings. A goal by Joe Juneau 28 seconds later slightly derailed them, but they recovered to close to 4-3 on Lapointe's goal at 8:08.

Doug Brown's goal at 15:46 of the third tied the score at 4.

"The third period was kind of a disaster for us," Capitals defenseman Mark Tinordi said. "They showed us why they're a championship team."

DANIEL MEARS

Esa Tikkanen got a dose of his own medicine from Joe Kocur.

Opposite page: Chris Osgood got a good look at a Capitals shot. Osgood made 29 saves.

Right: Not even the Great Motivator, Washington Caps Coach Ron Wilson, could find historical precedents to spur his troops to victory.

TOP: JACK GRUBER; BOTTOM: DANIEL MEARS

Brown's quick rush forces overtime

BY JERRY GREEN
The Detroit News

His nose was smashed across the bridge, bent out of shape, and blood from a gash smeared the middle of his red mustache grown for the playoffs.

"It's hockey," Doug Brown said in his Yankee twang, vintage New England, his nose puffy and possibly broken. "Part of the game."

It was a plugger's game. It was chock-full of muscle and grit, sudden momentum shifts and comebacks — and then the tingling suspense of sudden-death overtime.

Brown, with flair, created the ultimate suspense. With a flourish, he scored the goal that took Game 2 between the Red Wings and Washington Capitals into overtime. He rescued the Red Wings from defeat and embarrassment with just 4:14 left in regulation. He scored with a virtuoso effort, swiping the puck in the left faceoff circle and storming toward the goal to score.

Without that goal, there most likely would have been no tie, no overtime, no sudden-death goal by Kris Draper — the goal that won it for the Wings, 5-4.

"It's sort of nice to contribute," Brown said, "and find a way to win."

Very nice for the Red Wings, the reigning Stanley Cup champions, who have received much more of a competitive struggle from the Caps than most of these hockey savants and crystal-ball gazers thought possible.

The Wings are ahead in the Finals, two games to none, with the series to resume in Washington for games 3 and 4. But it could have been a two-games-to-none advantage for the underdog Capitals, if they had shot the puck a little straighter. And for much of the third period, it seemed the series would move to Washington with the teams even.

The Capitals twice had two-goal leads. They led 4-2, then 4-3. Then Doug Brown made it 4-4.

One of the pluggers.

He picked the puck out of two sets of Washington skates, turned and, with speed, skated toward Olaf Kolzig, the Caps goaltender. The shot beat Kolzig to his stick side.

And Brown went into a dance.

His goal capped the comeback, tied it, but Steve Yzerman's second goal, with the Wings shorthanded, started the comeback in the third period.

"Stevie was magnificent," Brown said of his locker neighbor. "Never mind the two goals, he almost had another half-dozen."

Brown spoke of the mood when the Red Wings went to their dressing room trailing 3-1 after the second period.

"We thought we had to play better," Brown said. "We weren't effective enough. We weren't doing smart things out there. We were a little frustrated."

More than a little.

Scotty Bowman watches his hockey team with his jaw raised, his face granite. He gives the impression that emotion is a weakness. When Draper scored and the Red Wings had won, Bowman lifted his right first in triumph and pounded the board partition behind him.

It was a rare display of emotion. And without a bit of Yankee ingenuity from Doug Brown, it would not have been possible.

DANIEL MEARS

The winning goal

Draper becomes latest unlikely hero

By JOHN NIYO

The Detroit News

So who had Kris Draper pegged to score the overtime goal? "If we threw our names in a hat, I don't think mine would have been the first one to come out," Draper said with a laugh after his goal — his first of the playoffs — finally ended Game 2 of the Stanley Cup Finals at 15:24 of overtime.

Draper? Anybody?

"I'm sure Mrs. Draper had Draper," Brendan Shanahan said, laughing.

But outside of family — and Draper did get a hug from his teary-eyed mother after the game — few would have picked him. Even after it was over, some people were still struggling with the truth.

"I have no idea who scored the winning goal," said Olaf Kolzig, the Washington goaltender who was beaten on the play. "Draper?"

Yes, Draper.

Draper, the only forward without a playoff goal for the Wings this spring, hopped off the bench to spell Igor Larionov moments before getting his grand opportunity, off an assist from Martin Lapointe.

"I came off a line change and I don't think anyone from Washington saw me," Draper said. "I was coming in back door and ... I just went to the net with my stick on the ice and (Lapointe) made a great pass and I just one-timed it into the open net."

From there, the rest is a blur. Draper's celebratory dance was best described as, well, unrehearsed. Scotty Bowman, in a rare show of emotion, pumped a fist in the air. Trainer John Wharton nearly injured himself in jubilation. Draper's teammates mobbed him along the boards — last but not least, his buddy Darren McCarty.

"What a time for him to get his first," McCarty said, shaking his head. "But it's funny, you know? Me and Drapes were sitting on the bench and I said to him, 'I think one of us is gonna get this.'"

Minutes later, Draper did. As goals go, it ranks pretty high on his list of accomplishments.

"This is it," he said, smiling from ear to ear at a news conference. "This is obviously my biggest goal. The only thing that can come close to it is the Western Conference finals

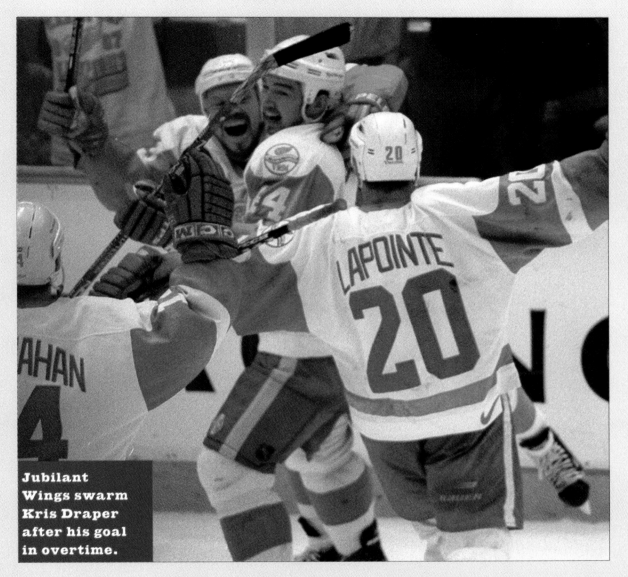

Jubilant Wings swarm Kris Draper after his goal in overtime.

ALAN LESSIG

(in 1995) when I got a game-winner against Chicago.

"I mean, this is what your dream is as a little kid. You know, playing ball hockey and the clock is counting down and you go to the open net and put it in for your team to win."

Fittingly, Thursday's game looked a bit like a ball hockey game with all the end-to-end action. The Wings, rallying to win from a two-goal deficit for the first time in these playoffs, tied it when Doug Brown lifted a shot past Kolzig with 4:14 remaining in regulation.

That set the stage for heroics, although no one

publicly volunteered.

"But guys were saying that the hero is going to be in this dressing room," said Draper, who missed the first three games of the playoffs rehabilitating a sprained knee.

Who would it be?

"It sounds like a broken record," McCarty said, "but different guys step up at different times on this team every game."

Said Steve Yzerman: "Our belief is that ... somehow somebody will score at some point."

Somebody did. And Kris Draper is one happy "somebody."

Exciting game just what hockey needs

By TERRY FOSTER

The Detroit News

Ladies and gentlemen of the press, we have a job to do. And we've got to snap to it before someone destroys this valuable piece of evidence.

Somewhere there is a secret memo from NHL Commissioner Gary Bettman demanding a game such as the one we saw in Game 2 at Joe Louis Arena. The Wings rallied for three goals in the third period, and Kris Draper ended this wild, crazy and stimulating game with an overtime goal that gave the Wings a 5-4 victory and a two-games-to-none lead in the Stanley Cup Finals.

How exciting was it? The ending made even stoic Scotty Bowman smile. It was so wonderful that even an elevator operator who did not see a second of the game knew something special was happening.

But this did not just happen. Somewhere there is a memo from Bettman demanding that these teams open the neutral zone and go at each other like a pair of wild rams protecting their territory.

Somewhere on NHL stationery, a memo says let the stars and goalies shine, let the muckers muck, and let every church bell ring to sound the game's praises.

I don't know if it is handwritten, typed or carved on a piece of slate. But somewhere there is a statement from Bettman screaming to let the pucks fly, let the fans cheer and let every American and Canadian see every ounce of skill from players such as Steve Yzerman and Peter Bondra.

This is what happens when the best skaters in the world are given enough room to make dramatic plays and horrific mistakes.

You get a frenzy more entertaining than Seinfeld ever dreamed of being.

It is our obligation in the press to find this memo, which I'm sure Bowman and Ron Wilson have fed to the paper shredder by now.

Can you believe the teams combined for 93 shots? Can you believe the action was so spellbinding that most of the fans actually stayed to the end?

Did you see Esa Tikkanen miss that wide-open net, Chris Osgood relax on Bondra's goal and the picture-perfect pass from Martin Lapointe to Draper?

"This is what NHL hockey is all about," Bettman said as the final seconds of regulation clicked off. "In terms of ebb and flow of the game, both teams are throwing everything they have at one another. From a spectator's point of view, this is a terrific game."

OK, Mr. Commish. Fess up. You orchestrated this. A day earlier, you were defending the game to reporters. When you said this remains the coolest game on ice, you should have seen the eyes roll.

When I jokingly suggested that Bettman orchestrated such a thriller, he laughed.

"I wish I could have done a better job of orchestrating the breakfast yesterday," he said. "It is so easy to accentuate the negative. But really, the positives outweigh the negatives. Most people, when they are able to watch our game, they react positively. People point to the ratings, but five years ago, our network television ratings were zero. So we are doing pretty good. I think what

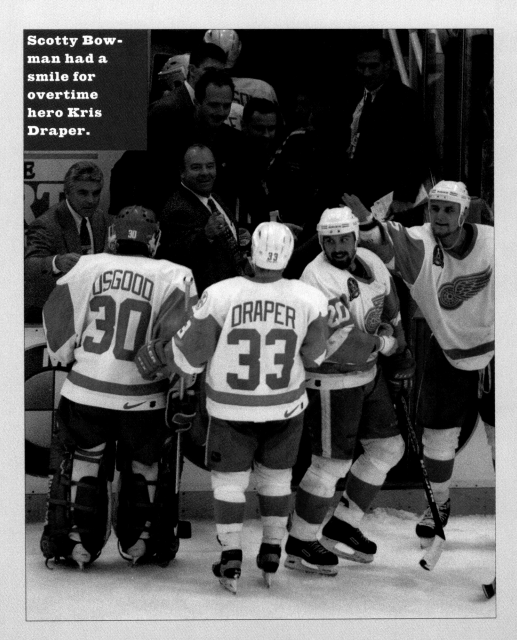

Scotty Bowman had a smile for overtime hero Kris Draper.

happens is people's expectations get set at a certain level. And we never promised anything in a approach which would equate with flipping a light switch. This is a slow process, and ultimately the game will sell itself."

It was so delicious, I felt like calling people who flick on playoff games this time of year only when Michael Jordan is playing and asking them to give this game a chance.

There must be a memo somewhere because Bettman promised that the series is just heating up.

"A series builds in intensity," he said. "By the time we got to the third period of the first game, it was a tight and competitive game. And that flowed right into this. This series should build in intensity."

Even more intense games? Hmmmm. I wonder if that was in the memo, too.

JACK GRUBER

Wings edge close to repeat

BY CYNTHIA LAMBERT

The Detroit News

T hree down, one to go. The Red Wings closed to within one victory of their second straight Stanley Cup after defeating the Washington Capitals, 2-1, in Game 3 at the MCI Center. Wings Coach Scotty Bowman also is a victory away from tying Toe Blake's coaching

WINGS	CAPITALS
1	0
0	0
1	1
2	1

JACK GRUBER

Sergei Fedorov's third-period goal thwarted the Caps.

The Wings knew the end was near, and so did the Capitals.

record of eight Stanley Cups.

The Wings lead the best-of-seven Finals series three games to none. A victory in Game 4 at the MCI Center would make the Wings the first team to repeat since the 1992 Pittsburgh Penguins, who also were coached by Bowman.

"Every game has been decided by one goal," Bowman said. "When you win three games by one goal. ... Tonight, it looked about just impossible to score any goals."

Improbable maybe, but not impossible. The Wings led 1-0 on Tomas Holmstrom's goal 35 seconds into the game. The lead lasted until 10:35 of the third period, when Brian Bellows popped a rebound past Chris Osgood.

At 15:09 of the third, Sergei Fedorov beat Olaf Kolzig for the winner, his first goal of the series and first in 11 games.

"No, I wasn't screened," Kolzig said. He then made a reference to a bonus clause in Fedorov's contract.

"I guess he just earned his 12 million bucks," Kolzig said.

Until that point, Kolzig had been outstanding and was the reason the Capitals were in the game. Chris Osgood was strong in net for the Wings, making 17 saves. Why such a low number? Well, the Capitals had just one shot in the first period.

"It was pretty easy (in the first period), to say the least," Osgood said. "I've found that whenever a team doesn't get a shot on net, that increases the chances that they're not going to score."

But there was more to the victory for the Wings than moving a step closer to repeating. It also was a time to remember a nightmare from June 13, 1997, when a limousine accident ended the careers of Vladimir Konstantinov and Sergei Mnatsakanov.

Before the game, Bowman told the players to say a prayer for Konstantinov and Mnatsakanov.

"What happened a year ago gives us extra motivation and extra inspiration to play," Fedorov said.

DANIEL MEARS

ALAN LESSIG

Charting the Red Wings' shots

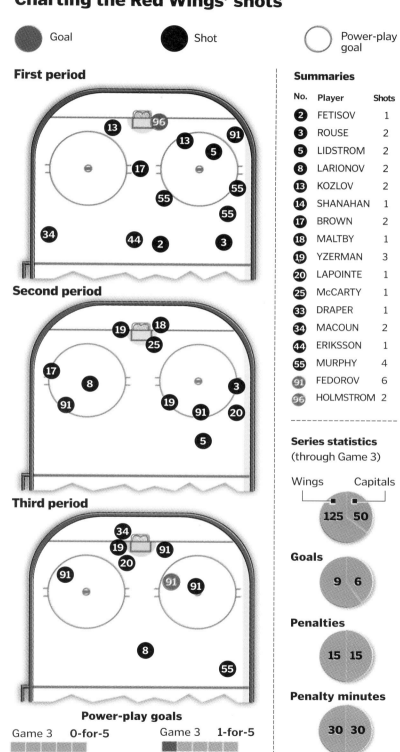

● Goal   ● Shot   ○ Power-play goal

First period

Second period

Third period

Power-play goals

Game 3   **0-for-5**   Game 3   **1-for-5**

Summaries

No.	Player	Shots
2	FETISOV	1
3	ROUSE	2
5	LIDSTROM	2
8	LARIONOV	2
13	KOZLOV	2
14	SHANAHAN	1
17	BROWN	2
18	MALTBY	1
19	YZERMAN	3
20	LAPOINTE	1
25	McCARTY	1
33	DRAPER	1
34	MACOUN	2
44	ERIKSSON	1
55	MURPHY	4
91	FEDOROV	6
96	HOLMSTROM	2

Series statistics
(through Game 3)

Wings   Capitals

125   **50**

Goals

9   **6**

Penalties

15   **15**

Penalty minutes

30   **30**

On verge of repeat

Red Wings perched on lip of another Cup

By BOB WOJNOWSKI

The Detroit News

They just keep driving, without regard for time or place, relentless in their pursuit of pucks and history. The Red Wings aren't waiting around any more, in a hurry, as if they've got somewhere important to be soon.

Who can stop them now? What can stop them now?

This time, it was Sergei Fedorov, breaking down the defense, beating Olaf Kolzig with just 4:51 remaining, giving the Wings a 2-1 victory over Washington. The Capitals and Kolzig have battled gamely, but they're just now discovering the odds. The Wings' victory gave them a three-games-to-none lead in the Stanley Cup Finals, one win from the sweetest of repeats.

The Wings are 7-0 in the Finals the last two years, and a victory in Game 4 would produce their second straight sweep. They're back at the lip of the Cup, pushed there by stars such as Fedorov, the $28-million man, and leaders such as Steve Yzerman, who set up the first goal.

And give another nod to Chris Osgood, who made big saves when necessary, although with Detroit playing its most stifling defense, it wasn't often necessary. The Capitals, for their infrequent offensive forays, were dangerous, as long as the Wings let them hang around.

The Wings made that mistake, and it nabbed them midway through the third period, on a power play, when Brian Bellows picked up a loose puck in front of Osgood and flipped it in, tying the game, 1-1.

But the Wings are nothing if not relentless.

They outshot and ouskated the Caps, and one goal was not about to derail them. Fedorov was brilliant for the second straight game, and when this season ends soon, he will be one of the major differences separating the champs from the chaff.

After the Wings had skated and scored and frolicked in a wild 5-4 overtime victory in Game 2, someone asked Yzerman if that's how they wanted to play.

"It's the way we like to play," he said, his straight face melting to a smile. "But our coach doesn't care for it."

Scotty Bowman likes defense. Bowman likes clamp-down, tight-checking hockey. Bowman likes to make the opposition look timid, frustrated and bored. So if the third period of Game 2 was like a salsa, this was back to a waltz. In the first period, the Wings' defense rode, broke and tamed the Capitals so thoroughly, the crowd spent the last two minutes booing the home team.

Washington's Mark Tinordi took a shot approximately 20 seconds into the game. And then, for the next 19:40, the Capitals looked like Pee-Wee Leaguers trying to stand on their skates and carry a stick at the same time. The Wings outshot 'em 13-1, and if not for Kolzig, the drama would have been over.

This is what the Wings do. Opponents think they have 'em figured out — So, they're going to open it up, huh? — and the Wings switch, back to the reliable, disciplined defense that can suffocate.

This is what champions do, beat you at your game, their game, any game. Of course, domination on the shot chart is not always reflected on the scoreboard, and the Wings again played dangerously, keeping the outmanned Caps in the game.

One shot per period won't accomplish much, and by the time the Caps unloaded their second shot three minutes into the second period, the Wings had a 16-1 edge. Impressive? Sure. Safe? Absolutely not.

Suddenly, there was Esa Tikkanen's slapper hitting a leg in front of Osgood, sliding ... sliding ... past Osgood, who was reaching ... reaching

back to snatch it before it crossed the line.

And for much of the game, that was the only thrill Washington's offense provided. Detroit's top defensive tandem of Nicklas Lidstrom and Larry Murphy was marvelous, as the Wings went back to the basics of boredom.

The Capitals came periodically to life, and in one stretch of the second period, Osgood was tremendous, twice stopping Bellows from point-blank range. The Capitals were dangerous on two

power plays, which meant the Wings leaned heavily on penalty-killer extraordinaire Yzerman.

Really, if last year's Cup quest was about ending the 42-year drought, this one seems to be whipped by the captain, who merely is playing as well as he ever has. He has a career-high 24 points in these playoffs and chases the puck as if it's the Cup itself. He has been there against every opponent, and his energy literally seems to push the Wings.

It was Yzerman who kept driving in the first minute, driving to the net, driving with Tikkanen on his back, driving into Kolzig, forcing the puck free to Tomas Holmstrom, who scored just 35 seconds into the game.

Yzerman always talks about the little things, then goes out and does them. He blocks shots. He wins faceoffs — 30-16 in the first two games, 6-1 in the first period of Game 3.

To repeat as champions, you need the wily experience, but you also need the wide-eyed drive, as if doing it for the first time. Somehow, Yzerman has kept both. His ego never intrudes, which makes it impossible for any egos on this team to grow unchecked.

No, the only thing growing is the ol' familiar hunger. Here comes Stanley again, closer and closer, and when these Wings reach for something, little can stop them. The Capitals know what they're up against now, too late to do anything about it.

The Wings have caught the scent — maybe they never lost the scent? — and taken aim. This championship is all but sealed, awaiting the final stamp, to be delivered soon, very soon.

DANIEL MEARS

Chris Osgood made big saves when necessary, and the Detroit defense was stifling.

Steve Yzerman carried the team, then the Cup.

Wings are sweeping sensations

Landslide in Washington clinches Stanley Cup

BY CYNTHIA LAMBERT
The Detroit News

For three games against the Washington Capitals, the Red Wings held their breath in one-goal games. In Game 4, they gave themselves ample breathing room and closed their second straight Stanley Cup with a 4-1 victory.

With 4.2 seconds to play, Larry Murphy skated with the puck to the left of the Red Wings goal, and goalie Chris Osgood threw his gloves and stick into the air in early celebration.

"I was going to shoot on him, but then I saw he didn't have his stick," Murphy said. "He was so happy, he couldn't stand it."

Osgood, a backup to Mike Vernon during last season's playoffs, was nearly speechless afterward.

"It was amazing," said Osgood, who was in goal for all 16 victories. "It was real emotional in the last minute, minute and a half. I couldn't wait.

"We went through a lot to get to that point. It was just amazing. I knew I could do it. I think I've

DANIEL MEARS

Olaf Kolzig couldn't stop Tomas Holmstrom and the Red Wings.

DANIEL MEARS

Charting the Red Wings' shots

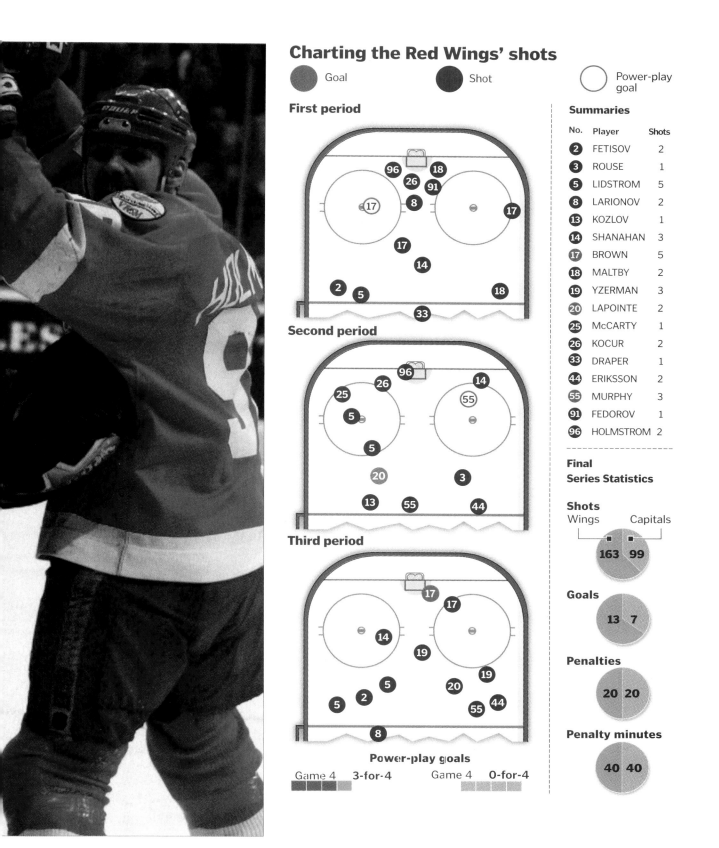

● Goal ● Shot ○ Power-play goal

First period

Second period

Third period

Power-play goals

Game 4 **3-for-4**

Game 4 **0-for-4**

Summaries

No.	Player	Shots
2	FETISOV	2
3	ROUSE	1
5	LIDSTROM	5
8	LARIONOV	2
13	KOZLOV	1
14	SHANAHAN	3
17	BROWN	5
18	MALTBY	2
19	YZERMAN	3
20	LAPOINTE	2
25	McCARTY	1
26	KOCUR	2
33	DRAPER	1
44	ERIKSSON	2
55	MURPHY	3
91	FEDOROV	1
96	HOLMSTROM	2

Final Series Statistics

Shots
Wings Capitals
163 99

Goals
13 7

Penalties
20 20

Penalty minutes
40 40

grown up 100 percent in these playoffs. I'm tougher now."

His team is, too.

The Wings are the first repeat Cup champions since the 1991 and 1992 Pittsburgh Penguins, and the first team to sweep consecutive Finals since the 1982 and 1983 New York Islanders. The Wings swept the Philadelphia Flyers last season.

The victory came with Vladimir Konstantinov watching from a private section of seats in the MCI Center. The Wings dedicated this season to Konstantinov and former team masseur Sergei Mnatsakanov. Both were injured in a limousine crash last June, six days after the Wings won their first Cup in 42 years.

"I don't think anyone can fully understand what this team went through," trainer John Wharton said. "The only thing I'm sad about is that Sergei couldn't be here for this. But because of the physical ramifications, he couldn't."

Steve Yzerman, in a unanimous vote, won the Conn Smythe Trophy as the playoff MVP.

"First of all, I can't believe I've won two Stanley Cups," Yzerman said. "I'm totally amazed by that. The Conn Smythe, I'm delighted to have my name on a significant trophy. It's great to have the Yzerman name on there along with my idols and my dad's idols."

The Wings have overcome a great deal this season, and Yzerman isn't their only hero.

"We lost to the defending champions, and they played like it," Washington goalie Olaf Kolzig said. "They deserved it."

The Wings' power play produced three goals — two by Doug Brown and one by Murphy. Martin Lapointe's even-strength goal early in the second period proved to be the winner.

Brown scored his first at 10:30 of the first period to give the Wings a 1-0 lead entering the second. In this postseason, the Wings were 13-1 when they scored the first goal.

Larionov and Murphy scored second-period goals, and in between Brian Bellows scored for the Capitals.

Red Wings forward Darren McCarty knows how to party: He showed off hockey's biggest prize to the MCI Center crowd during a victory lap after Game 4.

Brown capped it for the Wings with his second goal of the night and fourth of the playoffs.

"The goals can come pretty quick in hockey," Brown said. "That lead was nice, but we didn't want to let up. When they announced there was one minute left in the period, that's when I started getting excited."

The thrill won't end for some time. Winning back-to-back championships — in consecutive sweeps — is something special. And overcoming this season's adversity made it that much more gratifying.

"It was a different experience this year," Lapointe said. "We made it through lots of ups and downs. This team never quit. We always believed we could win.

"And don't write us off for next year. Don't you dare."

The Wings celebrated the way they played — as a united team.

For their friends

Vlady the inspiration behind Wings' repeat

By BOB WOJNOWSKI

The Detroit News

In a corner of the dressing room, secluded for a moment from the champagne-soaked madness, Igor Larionov bent to one knee, put his left arm around Vladimir Konstantinov and asked for a song.

"All right, Vlady, how about this one?" Larionov said, hugging him tightly, then gently beginning Vlady's favorite tune. "We ... are the champions ..."

And with the next line — "my friend" — Vlady began to sing, softly, hoarsely. He smiled and moved his head in rhythm, and for 10 wonderful seconds, it was two teammates sharing a victory, like it used to be, like it was supposed to be again.

So in the absence of a good beginning, or even a decent middle, there would be a splendid ending to a story that began a year and three days ago, a story alternately sad and uplifting. At the end of this Red Wings championship, capped by an overwhelming 4-1 victory and a sweep of Washington, there were so many scenes, so many moments, but even before Konstantinov was moved to sing, there was this: The team together again, on the ice in victory, pushing Konstantinov around in his wheelchair, clutching the Stanley Cup.

Perfect. On the final night, a team pushed all season by Konstantinov returned the favor, pushing back.

"That was something special," Larionov said. "I have goose bumps right now. Vlady has a chance to enjoy it this time. Everyone was so happy, but now I am a little sad. This guy should be playing with us."

Maybe he still was. It would be difficult to deny it, as player after player ran to Konstantinov's chair in the dressing room, lifted the Cup to his lips and begged him to drink. He usually obliged. And when trainer John Wharton dumped champagne on his head, Vlady jumped and smiled, his hair slicked back, two fingers held up, signifying back-to-back Cups.

The Wings finished back where they started, spurred by a simple word, one usually phrased as a question. Believe. Do you believe? The Wings turned it into a mandate, a quest, the ultimate reason to keep battling. And they discovered what others have found, that it is easier, when you believe.

It's the word they wore all season on their chests, on their hearts, on their sleeves. It's the word engraved on the stone in Konstantinov's locker, untouched since the accident more than a year ago. It's what the Wings had to feel as they leaped around the ice, then skated over, one by one, to bend down and hug Konstantinov, who sat with an unlit cigar in hand. Slava Fetisov, the only one in the limo to escape with his career intact, wept as they embraced.

When captain Steve Yzerman, the playoff MVP, presented the Cup to Konstantinov, eyes watered, and after months of pent-up emotion, you knew what it meant. This is not to forget masseur Sergei Mnatsakanov, also injured in the crash June 13, 1997, but unable to make the trip.

"We never tried to exploit the accident as a way of motivating our team," Yzerman said. "They're two really special guys for different rea-

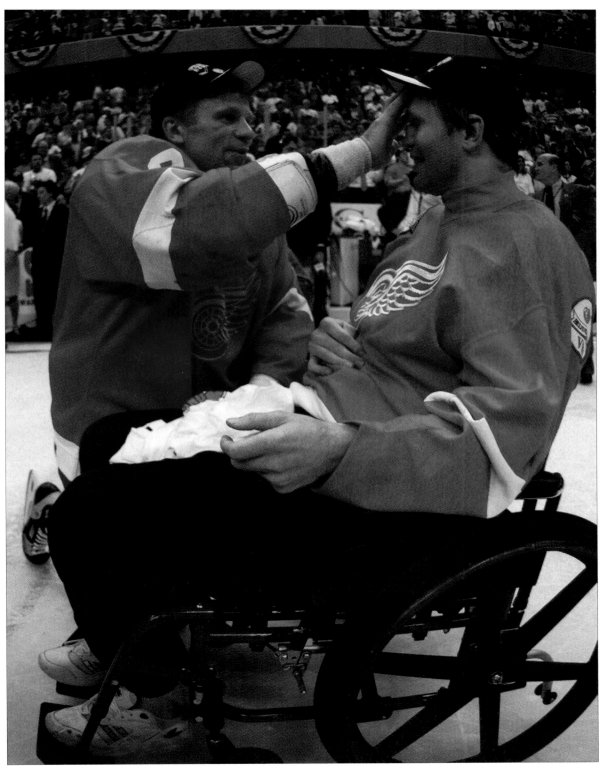

Comrades reunited in victory: Slava Fetisov and Vladimir Konstantinov shared a moment on the ice of the MCI Center after Game 4.

sons, really loved by the team. If anything, our team has grown closer through all this."

Something kept pushing these Wings, past obstacles and opponents, skating and grinding as if this game were the most important of their lives. In winning their second straight Cup and becoming the first repeat champion since Pittsburgh in 1991 and '92, the Wings shucked all shadows, and now take their place among the game's historical elite.

They did it with a volatile mix of discipline and emotion, defense and passion. Konstantinov watched from halfway up the MCI Center stands, just above a sign that read, "We believe — You believe." Huge pockets of Wings fans periodically burst into "Vla-dy!" chants, and dozens filed by his seat all game, clapping and thrusting fists, receiving a strong wave back.

This was about belief and much, much more. The champs, bonded by the accident, were led by their captain, who now assumes legendary status in Detroit sports lore. If the wounded players gave the Wings a cause, Yzerman and the wily coach, Scotty Bowman, pushed them. Bowman won his eighth Cup, tying Toe Blake's record, and here's hoping he sticks around to try to break it.

Yzerman got the validation he didn't really need, not from anyone who watched his passionate hockey during this two-month march to glory. He was named the Conn Smythe winner, and it was about a 20-way tie for second.

"I'm thrilled to have my name on a trophy that has some of the greatest names in hockey," Yzerman said. "When I came into the league, I don't think anybody knew how to spell my name, or pronounce it."

Spell it this way — Captain Cup. He's keeper of the hardware until someone dares take it away, and really, it won't be easy. The Wings have a spectacular gallery of stars, but they also have the league's best band of foot soldiers.

No one is under pressure to score because seemingly anyone can, at any time. There was Martin Lapointe, a sudden star, with his ninth

goal. There was Doug Brown, who reinjured a shoulder early in the playoffs, scoring twice, on perfect passes from Sergei Fedorov and Vyacheslav Kozlov.

There was Larry Murphy, a 37-year-old picture of persistence, ripping a goal past Olaf Kolzig. "Godzilla" had been the hottest goalie until he ran into a team that believed it couldn't be beat, not with its depth and its defense, not stalked by the image of its fallen warrior.

"This may sound cocky, but we were making plans for a party before this game," defenseman Bob Rouse said. "We just knew someone would step up when we needed them. We had everything going for us."

The Wings gathered momentum all season as they gathered perspective, and by the end, they were a red blur, scorching everything in their path. They thought they knew tragedy when they suffered a four-game humiliation against New Jersey. They thought they knew tragedy when hated Colorado crunched 'em, and Claude Lemieux laughed at the broken bones left behind.

Sports produces obstacles, life produces tragedies. So when the Wings lost two teammates, they found renewed purpose. Konstantinov and Mnatsakanov fought to carve a new life, a tougher life, and their teammates have never been the same.

"Everybody on this team looks at things totally different now," associate coach Dave Lewis said. "Resilience is a good word. That late goal against St. Louis? That's not devastating. A tough loss to Dallas? That's not devastating. We know what devastating is."

Would the Wings have repeated without the accident? Maybe. Probably. But who knows if lethargy would have seeped in. Who knows if Bowman, the Cup Master, would have been as determined to return.

Every day when players saw Vlady's locker, complacency was not an option. There is something poignantly ironic in that Konstantinov was the most indestructible Wing, the Vladinator, and

yet his body became an inflexible shell.

The Wings handled the situation with understated eloquence, so genuine it didn't need to be blared.

"The guys weren't trying to win it for them, because that doesn't make Vlady's and Sergei's lives any better," Wharton said. "They wanted to win it because of them. It was a silent rallying point, an internal thing."

It became external during these playoffs. The Wings could be wounded in strange ways, with a center-ice goal here, a blown lead there. But every opponent left with the same glazed look — Boy, they just don't crumble, do they?

You see it in Yzerman, once destined to spend a lifetime chasing something he couldn't have, now with more than many of the game's greats. You see it in Chris Osgood, who never buckled under the pressure of replacing Mike Vernon. Osgood is a symbol of the Wings' single-minded toughness, the ability to see past the noise. And yet for all this team's mental strength, it's easy to overlook the talent, four lines of endless energy.

The source of this passion? It starts with the leaders, the coach and the captain, who simply hate to lose.

It's fueled by the toughest team we've ever seen, incapable of being derailed, or distracted.

And then there are the real reasons to keep pushing, Vlady and Sergei, a couple of guys who didn't get to revel nearly long enough. If fate were fair, this celebration would last forever. This was for them, delivered by a team that never stopped believing it would sing again.

The burden of public scrutiny lifted, goalie Chris Osgood lept into the arms of teammate Martin Lapointe, another playoff hero.

While the Wings poured the bubbly, left, team owners Mike and Marian Ilitch took stock of the dividends of their investment.

TOP: JACK GRUBER; LOWER LEFT: ALAN LESSIG; LOWER RIGHT: DANIEL MEARS

Steve Yzerman: A
unanimous MVP choice.

Defenseman Bob Rouse and his son Torrey
talked to Bob's mom from the lockerroom.

Vladimir Konstantinov
and Slava Fetisov shared
the sweet taste of victory.

Wings' Captain Cup model of consistency

By DAVE DYE

The Detroit News

Last year, Red Wings fans wanted to see Steve Yzerman win the Stanley Cup, and he did.

This year, they wanted him to win the Conn Smythe Trophy, and he did that, too.

Yzerman, the captain, was named Most Valuable Player of the playoffs Tuesday night following a 4-1 victory over Washington that clinched the Wings' second straight Stanley Cup championship.

He was a unanimous selection.

Commissioner Gary Bettman called Yzerman "a great leader and a great player" as he presented the Conn Smythe to him.

Yzerman held it up, just as former Wing Mike Vernon did last year.

"I'm thrilled to have my name on a trophy that has some of the greatest names in hockey history," Yzerman said of the Conn Smythe. "When I came into the league, I don't think anybody knew how to spell my name or pronounce it. So I'm very proud the Yzerman name is going on a trophy that will be part of hockey for a long time.

"I haven't won anything in my career except the Cup, so this is very gratifying."

Yzerman, 33, said he was looking forward to just sitting on his couch and relaxing for a while.

"The playoffs are incredibly draining," he said. "I'm sick of wearing this uniform. I'm glad we won it tonight. I don't want to play another game."

Despite the exhaustion, Yzerman said he's never had more fun playing in his career.

"I want to play five more years," he said. "That's my goal. It's been the greatest time in my career, so I can't possibly think about not playing again."

Asked how he keeps playing as if he's still 25, Yzerman didn't hesitate with a rare one-liner.

"Viagra," he said.

Then he flashed that familiar toothless grin.

Yzerman was held without a point Tuesday in Game 4, but he still led the league in playoff points with 24 (six goals, 18 assists). It was the most productive playoff in Yzerman's 15-year NHL career.

He was the heart and soul of a team that has a lot of heart and a lot of soul.

Yzerman was a model of consistency throughout the playoffs. He scored big goals. He made big passes. He killed penalties. He won faceoffs. He forechecked. He backchecked. He blocked shots. He put his superstar status aside and played the grinder's role when necessary.

"He did it all," teammate Kirk Maltby said.

Said Doug Brown: "You don't want to let (Yzerman) down because you know how much heart he's given to the team."

In reality, Yzerman's Conn Smythe was in the making for several years. His transformation from a scorer to a well-rounded player is a big reason the Wings have won consecutive titles.

For the series, Yzerman dominated on faceoffs.

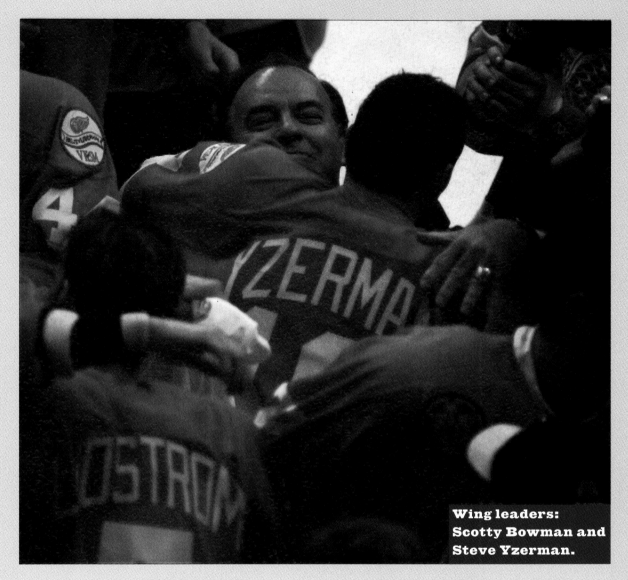

Wing leaders:
Scotty Bowman and
Steve Yzerman.

He won 62 of 93 (66.6 percent).

"Stevie plays well at both ends of the rink," Capitals Coach Ron Wilson said. "He's their most consistent player. He deserves the award."

The series started a week ago Tuesday with Yzerman getting pushed around by Dale Hunter. At one point, Hunter rubbed Yzerman's face in the ice.

"He took quite a beating in Game 1," Wings Coach Scotty Bowman said. "I think that got him really geared up to beat them with his stick and skates. He's not the type to try to beat you with his fists.

"I give a lot of credit to Steve Yzerman. He didn't complain after the first game. He came up with big plays all series."

Yzerman said that after the Wings won the Cup last year, he thought he would be happy without ever winning again.

"But when the playoffs came around, you could tell everybody wanted to win just as bad," he said. "You don't lose your desire to win after one. We had a taste and wanted to win again. It's really satisfying."

Especially when it comes with a Conn Smythe Trophy, too.

Almost too good to believe: The Wings, with team inspiration Vladimir Konstantinov, put the Stanley Cup on ice following a 4-1 victory in Game 4.

DANIEL MEARS